DISUSED STATIONS
Closed Railway Stations In the UK

Lost Stations of
Northumberland & Durham

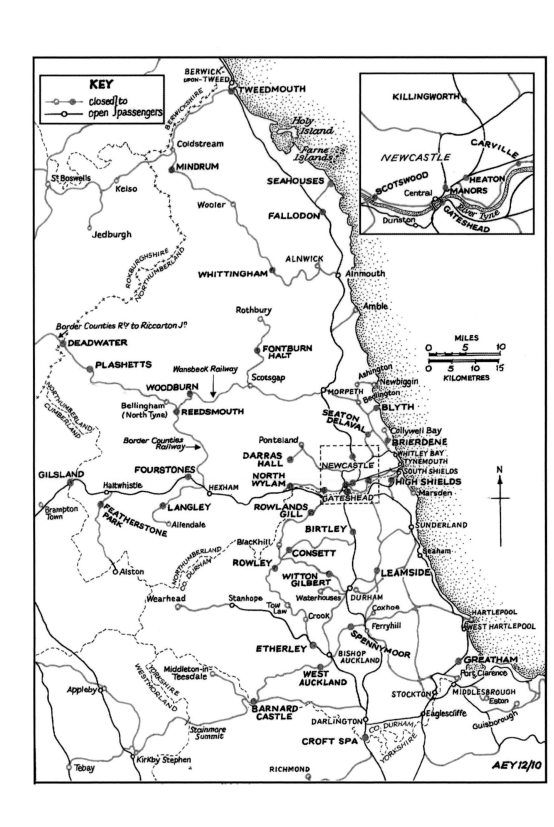

DISUSED STATIONS
Closed Railway Stations In the UK

Lost Stations of Northumberland & Durham

Alan Young

Silver Link Publishing Ltd

British Library Cataloguing in Publication Data

A catalogue record for this book is available from the British Library.

ISBN 978 1 85794 377 1

Silver Link Publishing Ltd
The Trundle
Ringstead Road
Great Addington
Kettering
Northants NN14 4BW

Tel/Fax: 01536 330588
email: sales@nostalgiacollection.com
Website: www.nostalgiacollection.com

Printed and bound in the Czech Republic

First published in 2011

Please note:
Silver Link Publishing Ltd (Silver Link) is not responsible for the content of external websites. The reasons for this are as follows:
> Silver Link does not produce them or maintain/update them and cannot change them.
> Such sites can be changed without Silver Link's knowledge or agreement.

Where external links are given they may be to websites which also offer commercial services, such as online purchasing. The inclusion of a link or links to a website(s) in our books should not be taken or understood to be an endorsement of any kind of that website(s) or the site's owners, their products or services.

Cover illustrations:
Background: **Carville** in December 1972. Alan Young
Front top: **Reedsmouth** in 1953. Colour Rail
Front lower left: **Manors North** in March 1972. Alan Young
Front lower right: **Seaton Delaval** in December 1972. Alan Young

The Author - Alan Young

Alan was born in Newcastle upon Tyne in 1951. At first he lived in Heaton, then spent his school years in Longbenton. In 1969, after completing his A-levels at George Stephenson Grammar School, West Moor, he read geography at Fitzwilliam College, Cambridge. For almost 40 years Alan taught geography, working in Hertfordshire, London and Lancashire, but having retired from teaching he is now a Tour Manager for a railway holiday travel firm.

While most railway enthusiasts collected engine numbers, Alan's interest was always in the infrastructure, particularly stations. His first taste of stations was on the 'Coast Circle' route (now part of the Tyne & Wear Metro system), which probably had the greatest variety of stations on any suburban route in Britain, ranging from the magnificent Newcastle Central, through the large and impressive Tynemouth, Manors and Whitley Bay, to the charm of South Gosforth's almost rural station, and the classic 'inner-city' Heaton, the station that triggered his interest.

Alan's passionate interest in geography developed as he became an avid collector of Ordnance Survey maps; then, starting with his purchase of a North Eastern Region timetable in 1962, he began to plan journeys to visit the area's lines and stations. Thanks to a level of trust that parents seldom have in their children today, Alan was given the freedom to use Runabout and 'day line' tickets, so he could travel on routes that were soon to disappear as the Beeching closures took effect. His station photography began at Blencow on the old Penrith-Keswick line, but it gathered momentum in the early 1970s; disappointed at being just too late to record the South Shields branch stations before their modernisation, he set out to visit all stations, past and present, in Great Britain and Ireland, and to photograph them in colour.

In 1974 Alan's first article (on the Newcastle-Tynemouth Riverside branch) was published in Railway World, and he was able to share his interest in disused stations in 'A British closed stations safari' published in The Railway Magazine in 1980. He has also written or contributed to books on railway architecture, private and untimetabled stations, British Railways station totems, railway poster art, and the history of Tyneside and Northumberland railways. For some time he has supplied articles and photographs to the 'Disused Stations' website, for which he is also the cartographer, and he provides support in editing and proof-reading material submitted for the website.

Contents

Acknowledgements

I am grateful for the generous help I have received from a number of people while preparing this book: Nick Catford, for having the enterprise and energy to set up the 'Disused Stations' website, and working to enhance the quality of some of the photographs; Martin Bairstow, for information on LNER and BR camping coaches; Jonathan Clark, for sharing his knowledge of Gateshead and Spennymoor stations and commenting constructively on the Manors section; Christopher Dean, for information on railways in the Seaton Sluice area; David Dunn, for tracking down elusive photographs of Killingworth racecourse sidings; Richard Furness, for supplying photographs of station totem signs; Brian Johnson, for information on and photographs of West Auckland, and photographs of several other stations; Roy Lambeth, for sharing some of his extensive knowledge of north-eastern railways, notably Etherley and West Auckland; Ed Orwin, for providing a portfolio of photographs and information on the Blyth & Tyne Railway for me to study, and for adding details to the Blyth and Seaton Delaval sections; Peter Singlehurst, for detailed information about West Auckland station; Michael Stewart, who has supplied the tickets from his extensive collection*; Les Turnbull, for his encouragement and for giving permission to use a number of his photographs; Paul Wright, who, as author of companion Silver Link volumes, has given advice and encouragement; and finally to the late John Mann, whose collection of more than 60,000 station photographs was donated to the 'Disused Stations' website in 2010, and some of which illustrate this book.

* *Publisher's note:* Paul Wright the author of the previous volume in the series: *Lost Stations of North West England* has asked that his appreciation of Michael Stewart's contribution of tickets for inclusion in that volume also be recorded.

Bibliography

Addyman, John F. and Mallon, John *The Alnwick & Cornhill Railway* (NERA, 2007)

Addyman, John F. (ed) *A History of the Newcastle & Berwick Railway* (NERA, 2011)

Biddle, Gordon *Victorian Stations* (David & Charles, 1973)
Britain's Historic Railway Buildings (Oxford University Press, 2003)

Bowtell, Harold D. *Dam Builders' Railways from Durham's Dales to the Border* (Plateway Press, 1994)

Bragg, S. and Scarlett, E. *North Eastern Lines and Stations* (NERA, 1999)

Clinker, C. R. *Register of Closed Passenger Stations and Goods Depots* (Avon Anglia, 1978)

Cook, R.A. and Hoole, Ken *North Eastern Railway Historical Maps* (RCHS, 2nd edition, 1991)

Croughton, Godfrey, Kidner R. W. and Young, Alan *Private and Untimetabled Stations* (Oakwood Press, 1982)

Fawcett, Bill *A History of North Eastern Railway Architecture* (3 volumes) (NERA, 2001-05)
A History of the Newcastle & Carlisle Railway 1824-70 (NERA 2008)

Gibbins, E.A. *The Railway Closure Controversy* (Leisure Products, 2000)

Godfrey, Alan *Old Ordnance Survey maps* (various)

Hoole, Ken *A Regional History of the Railways of Great Britain: Vol 4 The North East* (David & Charles, 2nd edition, 1974)
Railway Stations of the North East (David & Charles, 1985)

Introduction

Northumberland and Durham can claim to be the counties that gave railways to the world. From the early 17th century, in the 'Great Northern Coalfield' wagonways were built to move the coal to tidal water for export, and by 1800 there was an intricate network of these routes. The genius of George Stephenson, a native of Northumberland, was applied to developing efficient steam traction and to engineering the Stockton & Darlington Railway, the first public railway in the world to operate steam-hauled passenger trains at its opening in 1825. The first line across England to connect the navigable waters of the west and east coasts was the Newcastle & Carlisle Railway, which opened to passengers between 1835 and 1839. By the close of the 19th century the coalfield had acquired a dense network of passenger railways, but lines also threaded their way through sparsely populated countryside, reaching such remote villages as Bellingham and Wearhead. A number of companies built the counties' lines, but by 1874 much of the system was under the wing of the North Eastern Railway. A delightful eccentricity of Northumberland's network was that 74 miles of its lines were owned and operated by the Scottish company, the North British Railway. Were it not for competition with the NER, these unprofitable North British lines might never have been completed.

The railway system of Northumberland and Durham reached its fullest extent by 1914. After the First World War competition from motor buses, cars and lorries drew traffic away from the railways. At first the response of the London & North Eastern Railway was to exercise minor economies, such as closing ticket offices at its quietest stations, but in 1930 more drastic measures were taken, in which almost a fifth of Northumberland's passenger network was closed: this included the Alnwick to Coldstream route – at 35¾ miles, the longest stretch of line to have closed in Britain. United, which appeared to lead the motor bus competition on the roads, was an associated company of the LNER, and this undoubtedly encouraged the railway company to withdraw its least remunerative train services. In the late 1930s some lines in western County Durham lost their passenger services.

Under the administration of the nationalised British Railways, closures resumed. In the 1950s most closures affected quieter rural lines (such as the Wearhead branch and the ex-North British system), but the Durham coalfield was also included, where bus competition was intense. Minor stations on the East Coast Main Line also closed in that decade. By the time that *The Reshaping of British Railways* (the 'Beeching Report') was published in March 1963 many stations in Northumberland and Durham were already lost, but it recommended further closures such as the Blyth, Newbiggin and Riverside branches in Northumberland, Sunderland to Bishop Auckland, and Darlington to Richmond, Middleton-in-Teesdale, and Crook. Of these lines

Hurst, Geoffrey *Register of Closed Railways 1948-1991* (Milepost Publications, 1992)

Jenkins, Stanley C. *The Alston Branch* (Oakwood Press, 1991)
The Rothbury Branch (Oakwood Press 1991)

Quick, Michael *Railway Passenger Stations in Great Britain: A Chronology* (RCHS, 2009)

Sewell, G. W. M. *The North British Railway in Northumberland* (Merlin, 1992)

Sinclair, Neil T. and Carr, Ian S. *Railways of South Shields* (Tyne & Wear Museums, 1990)

Teasdale, J. G. (ed) *A History of British Railways' North Eastern Region* (NERA, 2009)

Turnbull, Les *Tickets not Transferable* (Ergo Press, 2007)

Walton, Peter *The Stainmore and Eden Valley Railways* (OPC, 1992)

Warn, C. R. *Railways of the Northumberland Coalfield* (Frank Graham, 1976)

Wells, J. A. *The Blyth & Tyne Railway* (3 volumes) (Northumberland County Library, 1989-91)

Whittle, G. *The Railways of Consett and North-West Durham* (David & Charles, 1971)

Wright, Alan *The North Sunderland Railway* (Oakwood Press, 2nd edition, 1988)

Young, Alan *Suburban Railways of Tyneside* (Martin Bairstow, 1999)
Railways in Northumberland (Martin Bairstow, 2003)

Hansard (various) (HMSO)
North Eastern Express North Eastern Railway Association (various)

only the Darlington-Bishop Auckland section of the Crook line was reprieved. Few lines and stations have closed since 1970, but passenger services on the Riverside branch ceased in 1973, while the Haltwhistle-Alston branch, already listed for closure before 'Beeching', succumbed in 1976. A few stations (such as Heaton and High Shields) were sacrificed when the network was reorganised in the Tyne & Wear Metro project, but new ones were added.

In Northumberland and Durham there are more than 200 closed stations. In the urban and industrial areas most have been demolished, with their sites redeveloped: these are the truly 'lost' stations. In the countryside, however, there are many delightful disused stations. On the Alnwick-Coldstream and Durham-Blackhill lines, for instance, the substantial villas provided for the North Eastern Railway station masters remain in occupation at most of the stations, and the same is true for many of the Hexham-Riccarton Junction North British stations. Even on the East Coast Main Line and between Newcastle and Carlisle some disused station buildings survive, many years after they closed.

This book is a companion to the popular 'Disused Stations' website, which now features more than 1,500 locations. Some of the stations included here are to be found on the website, while others are new. They are arranged in chronological order of opening, beginning with a station on the Stockton & Darlington Railway, and ending with one that would have opened in 1914 had it not been for the outbreak of the First World War. It is hoped that the collection here will illustrate the wide variety of disused stations in Northumberland and Durham, whether they can still be seen today or have been erased from the landscape.

Key to headings:

STATION NAME	Indicates station closed to passengers pre-nationalisation
STATION NAME	Indicates station closed to passengers post-nationalisation
STATION NAME	Indicates station closed to passengers post-privatisation

Note on Counties used

This book locates the individual station sites within the counties that existed prior to the local government reorganisation that took place on 1 April 1974. In fact, the counties and boundaries that were set in 1974 were for the purposes of creating administrative districts, and the historic counties were not altered.

In recent years many of the 1974 County Councils have themselves been swept away, confusing the situation even further. The author felt therefore that using the historic county names would be easier for the reader.

Note on Ordnance Survey extracts

These are provided for stations that are not included in the Disused Stations website.

WEST AUCKLAND (1833 and 1858)

First station opened	December 1833
Location	Station Road/Manor Road, south-east of former level crossing
Company on opening	Stockton & Darlington Railway
Date closed to passengers	February 1847
Date closed completely	February 1847
Company on closing	Stockton & Darlington Railway
Present state	No evidence remains
County	Durham
OS Grid Ref	NZ185266

West Auckland is an attractive village that retains a rural quality in spite of former coal-mining in the vicinity and its more recent development as a commuter settlement for Bishop Auckland.

The first station here was named St Helens (or St Helens

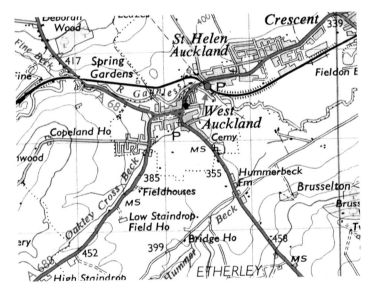

West Auckland: Looking east from the level crossing, the West Auckland colliery line is the one on the left. The unusual layout can be seen, with both platforms facing in the same direction. *John Mann collection*

Second station opened	13 October 1858
Location	Station Road/Manor Road, south-east of former level crossing
Company on opening	Stockton & Darlington Railway
Date closed to passengers	18 June 1962
Date closed completely	18 June 1962
Company on closing	British Railways (North Eastern Region)
Present state	Demolished. A grassy area and path follow the trackbed through the station site. The station house survives.
County	Durham
OS Grid Ref	NZ185266

Auckland) after the village that adjoins West Auckland. For some years it was the northern terminus of the Stockton & Darlington Railway, the first public railway in the world to operate steam-hauled passenger trains at its opening. Having used steam haulage from Shildon, through Darlington, to Stockton on 27 September 1825 – the ceremonial opening day – regular passenger trains were introduced on 10 October, but only between Stockton and Darlington, and drawn by horses. The passenger service was extended to Shildon in April 1826. Coal trains had operated from Witton Park Colliery (Etherley) through St Helens Auckland to Stockton from September 1825, but passenger trains were not extended to St

Helens until December 1833 (and onward to Lands, on the Haggerleases branch, from April 1834). The service was horse-drawn from St Helens (and Lands) to the Brusselton Inclines. A stationary engine hauled the coach up, then lowered it down, the inclines, after which it was attached to a steam-hauled coal train and continued to Darlington (regular steam services having been introduced two months earlier). It is thought that the difficulty of working over the inclines prompted the company to replace the trains with a horse omnibus service from South Church (Bishop Auckland) in 1842, coinciding with the opening of a new route through Shildon Tunnel. However, a market train for Darlington is thought to have continued

West Auckland: A passenger train for Bishop Auckland enters the station. The footbridge, installed in 1913, gave access to the original platform and booking office. *W. A. Camwell*

to operate on alternate Mondays. Bradshaw shows that the service was restored in January 1843, and it continued until February 1847, after which the bus service was resumed.

The convention of providing a platform and formal station buildings with booking facilities where passengers joined and left the trains was a thing of the future: 'stopping places' were generally where the railway crossed roads, and passengers using the Stockton & Darlington obtained their tickets at nearby inns, such as the Mason's Arms and Grey Horse Inn at Shildon. Thus at St Helens Auckland there was no platform for the horse-drawn service, but, since this was the terminus, there was a coach house to accommodate the passenger vehicle.

The second station on the site was also known as St Helens, but it was renamed West Auckland on 1 March 1878. Initially its passenger service operated between Bishop Auckland and Lands, reversing at Tunnel Junction (immediately north of Shildon Tunnel), but from 1 August 1863 the need for the reversal ceased when a new direct line from Bishop Auckland to St Helens (Fieldon Bridge Junction) opened.

The second station had a remarkable layout. On the double-track route the eastbound platform (for Bishop Auckland) was sandwiched between the two tracks, rather like an island platform, but it was fenced and its building

West Auckland: A general view of the station from the signal box on 3 March 1962. The station house can be seen in the distance, beyond the waiting shelter. Brian Johnson

extended to the back of the platform. The up platform (for Barnard Castle) was in the normal flanking position, but faced the back of the down platform: this original single platform and building were on the south side of the double-track line. There were several other stations in North East England with this arrangement of a single platform on a double-track, such as Etherley, described in a later chapter. Such a layout required all stopping passenger trains in one direction to cross over to the other line, which proved inconvenient when traffic increased. At some time before 1896 the second platform was constructed. There was a problem in placing this platform as, in addition to the double-track, a third line serving West Auckland Colliery passed north of the main tracks, and a cross-over track between the colliery line and the main lines was required, which would also rule out the siting of the new platform in a conventional position. Moreover, if the new platform were north of the running lines, passengers would have to cross two tracks on the level at a location where visibility along the line in both directions was very restricted. By placing the new platform between the two main tracks, passengers would have only one track to cross to reach the booking office. A further option of building a new 'staggered' platform further east, beyond the point where the colliery line joined the main line, was probably ruled out as more land would have to be purchased to the north, and an underbridge east of the station would need to be widened. Thus the new platform was sandwiched between the

West Auckland: Signalman Trevor Lee closes the crossing gates on 3 March 1962. In the distance can be seen the pit-heap of West Auckland Colliery, which closed in 1967. *Brian Johnson*

Durham and Ulverston on alternate Fridays, did stop at West Auckland.

Diesel multiple units were introduced on 16 September 1957, by which time the local service had declined to two trains each way. On 15 September 1958 West Auckland lost its goods service, and Cockfield Fell closed to passengers: Evenwood had closed in 1957. West Auckland's passenger service was also reduced to one train each way: the 8.41am (Monday-Friday only) to Bishop Auckland, and the 4.21pm in the opposite direction met the needs of girls attending Bishop Auckland Grammar School. A morning train westbound and an evening eastbound working did not stop at West Auckland. Only a few months after the highly publicised and much lamented closure of the neighbouring Stainmore route from Barnard Castle to Penrith, passenger services through West Auckland ended much more discreetly on 18 June 1962.

West Auckland's goods yard trackwork was lifted in October 1959, but mineral traffic continued to operate through the station, after passenger closure, to West Auckland Washery and Randolph Coke Works at Evenwood. On 10 April 1965 the signal box closed and 'one train working' on the up line was introduced, with the train crew operating the crossing gates. The down line through the station was lifted in July 1965, and the signal box was dismantled later that year. In August 1968 the passenger station platforms and buildings were demolished. The line through West Auckland closed entirely on 2 September 1968; West Auckland Washery had closed in August 1967, and Randolph Coke Works ceased working on 30 August 1968 (though it reopened, served by road, from December 1968 until May 1984). In March 1970 the up line was lifted, leaving only the station master's house, which is still in use.

tracks, and a footbridge to the other platform was installed in 1913.

The station house stood beyond the south-east end of the Barnard Castle platform. The platform buildings were austere, single-storey brick structures, the main facilities being in the earlier westbound platform building. The goods warehouse was west of the crossing, and the principal traffic was bricks, creosote, tar, pitch and manure.

In 1911 West Auckland booked 51,061 passengers, and it was estimated that the station served approximately 6,000 people. Its train service in June 1920 amounted to six each way on weekdays only between Barnard Castle and Bishop Auckland, and they also called at Cockfield (renamed Cockfield Fell in 1923) and Evenwood, the other two stations on the line. The June 1943 timetable shows a reduction to four trains on weekdays, with five on Saturdays. On summer Saturdays trains between the North East and Lancashire coast resorts used the line but did not call at West Auckland. However, the unadvertised Durham Convalescent Miners' trains, which ran between

West Auckland: The final timetabled passenger train, the 4.21pm departure for Bishop Auckland, enters the station on 16 June 1962. *Brian Johnson*

Below **West Auckland:** On 13 October 1962 the 'Durham Railtour' visits the station. The signal box and crossing can be seen in the background. *Roy Lambeth*

Bottom left **West Auckland:** Looking south-east in February 2011. The railway tracks and platforms occupied the strip of grass, while the former station house is in the distance. *Alan Young*

Right **West Auckland:** The former station house in February 2011. *Alan Young*

Below **West Auckland:** A map of the surrounding railway network and stations, past and present. *Alan Young*

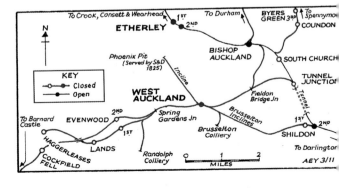

GILSLAND (Probably 1836)

Date opened	Probably 19 July 1836
Location	On the Newcastle to Carlisle railway in Gilsland village, immediately south-west of the railway bridge
Company on opening	Newcastle & Carlisle Railway
Date closed to passengers	2 January 1967
Date closed completely	2 January 1967
Company on closing	British Rail (Eastern Region)
Present state	The platforms have been demolished. The main station building and former waiting room block are in residential use.
County	Northumberland
OS Grid Ref	NY636664

Gilsland village straddles the border of Northumberland and Cumbria (formerly Cumberland) and is close to Hadrian's Wall. Before the coming of the railway the village was noted for its sulphur and chalybeate spa waters. In 1797 Walter Scott visited the resort, apparently looking for a wife, and a French emigrée whom he met there proved acceptable.

The station was on the first line to cross England between navigable waters of the west and east coasts. The Newcastle & Carlisle Railway received the Royal Assent on 22 May 1829 and opened in stages between 1834 and 1838. From the east the route followed the South Tyne, then the valley of the Tipalt Burn, and close to Gilsland it used a low watershed to enter the valley of the Irthing, the river on which Gilsland is found. Beyond here the railway should logically have continued in the Irthing valley, but pressure from

a major landowner, and from the people of Brampton, who thought the railway would be detrimental to its economy, forced the railway southward into hillier country where construction was difficult and expensive. The N&C opened to passengers from Blaydon to Hexham on 10 March 1835, then eastwards to Derwenthaugh on 11 June and westwards to Haydon Bridge on 28 June of that year. On 19 July 1836 the route from Carlisle through Gilsland to Blenkinsopp Colliery (near Haltwhistle) opened. The line pushed further

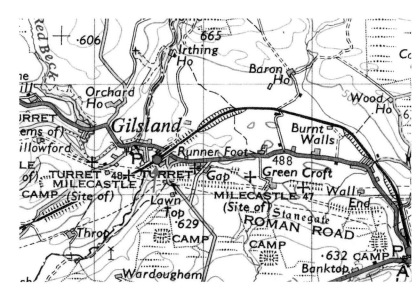

Gilsland: In this undated view looking towards Newcastle the platform roofing, installed in 1902 by the North Eastern Railway, can be seen. On the Carlisle-bound (right-hand) platform was one of the distinctive waiting sheds that were provided at many Newcastle & Carlisle stations, accompanied by a North Eastern Railway signal box. *Alan Young collection*

east to Redheugh (Gateshead) on 1 March 1837, passengers for Newcastle having to use a ferry across the River Tyne to a temporary 'station' at No 66 The Close. On 15 June 1838 the full length of the line from Gateshead to Carlisle opened. From 21 October 1839 a regular service to Newcastle was introduced using a temporary bridge at Scotswood. The Newcastle terminus at the Shot Tower was replaced with one at Forth on 1 March 1847, and from 1 January 1851 N&C trains used Central station, shared with the York, Newcastle & Berwick Railway.

Gilsland station opened as Rose Hill – its name until 1 May 1869 – and was a mile south of the spa. The pioneering N&C saw no need for platforms, but did construct charming

station houses; at Gilsland it was north-west of the tracks, well set back, which proved advantageous when a platform was added. The architect was probably John Blackmore, who held a senior engineering post in the N&C and was latterly Chief Engineer. No shelters were provided for passengers, who probably huddled together in the station master's front room, where tickets were sold. Gilsland and the other stations received what was known at the time as Modern Gothic buildings, with Tudor elements such as mullioned windows and hood-moulds, but with sash windows rather than the traditional casements. Construction was of sandstone, and the building was single-storey with an attic whose cross-gable window rested on shapely wooden corbels. No doubt in recognition of the numbers of visitors to the genteel spa, the N&C added a further waiting room block south-west of the station building, its design complementing the original, as well as a restrained, but elegant, glazed iron verandahh that fronted both buildings. In NER days a booking office window was added to the platform elevation of the main building, and the glazed verandah was replaced in 1902 with corrugated iron roofing. This ugly structure obscured the attractive building, but its 26ft 6in span and partial end-screen sheltered more passengers. In 1910 crudely designed dormers appeared each side of the cross-gable. On the opposite platform were a signal box and a stone,

pent-roof waiting shed, its front enclosed by wood and glass. The NER platform roof was removed long before the station closed, but columns that carried it remained as posts for oil lanterns. The platforms were connected by a subway.

In 1907 Gilsland issued 20,710 tickets, but excursions brought many more passengers

through its doors. By 1951 only 1,494 tickets were sold, and excursion visits were few since the spa had closed. In the summer of 1955 the service consisted of nine weekday (three Sunday) trains to Newcastle and seven weekday (four Sunday) trains to Carlisle.

Gilsland was one of 13 Newcastle-Carlisle stations proposed for closure by Beeching. The Transport Users' Consultative Committee report of 18 February 1966 noted British Railways' claim that these closures would allow accelerated diesel multiple unit services and increase the DMU fleet's productivity by integrating these 'express' services with Newcastle-Hexham local workings. Gilsland's closure attracted objections, some undoubtedly justified, others speculative or exaggerated. Claims that visitors to the convalescent home – the former spa – would be inconvenienced were dismissed because not a single visitor in 1965 had come by train. Likewise 'about fifteen teenagers' dependent on Saturday evening trains for entertainment in Carlisle were found, in BR's census, to be 'about three'. A protestor was aggrieved by the retention of Brampton Junction, 'nearly two miles from the town, used by virtually no passengers, and with half-hourly buses to Carlisle', while Gilsland was proposed for closure. BR responded that Brampton was 'retained as a central point', but its future would depend on the level of use.

Gilsland's goods facilities closed on 5 April 1965. Passenger trains ceased to call on 2 January 1967, and the platforms and down platform shelter were dismantled, but the up-side buildings survive.

Gilsland: In August 2001 the original station house (right) with the later waiting room block (left) survived. Both were constructed by the Newcastle & Carlisle Railway. *Alan Young*

FOURSTONES (Probably 1837)

Date opened	Probably January 1837
Location	On the Newcastle to Carlisle railway. Reached by the lane leading southwards at the crossroads (B6319) in Fourstones.
Company on opening	Newcastle & Carlisle Railway
Date closed to passengers	2 January 1967
Date closed completely	2 January 1967
Company on closing	British Rail (Eastern Region)
Present state	The platforms and 1879/80 buildings have been demolished. The original station building is in residential use.
County	Northumberland
OS Grid Ref	NY891677

The pleasant village of Fourstones is on the north bank of the South Tyne just over 2 miles west of its confluence with the North Tyne. From 1805 until 1927 Fourstones had a coal mine, employing no more than 120 men throughout its life. The small scale of this colliery, and others in the upper Tyne valleys, meant that it did not encourage the development of sprawling grid-pattern terraces found further east in the Northumberland and Durham coalfield. However, until the 1970s the old colliery imposed itself on the landscape by virtue of a small pit-heap and siding west of the station.

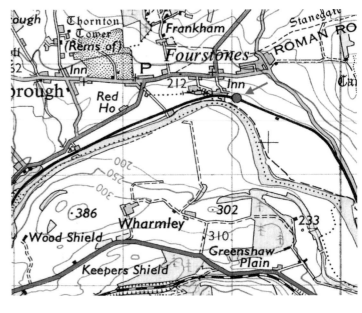

Fourstones station was on the Newcastle to Carlisle line, whose history has been described in the Gilsland chapter above, and it replaced two short-lived stations, Warden to its east and Allerwash to its west. The actual opening date is unclear because Bradshaw timetables did not list all of the N&C stations until 1848, but other documentary evidence suggests that it opened in 1837. The original station house, set back from the up line, was a dignified, single-storey

affair. It was completed in 1839, and was the smallest N&C station building, although it was later extended. It had a T-plan with a large, round bay facing the track, which housed the booking office. The distinctive style was chosen either because this station was used by John Clayton, legal advisor to the N&C and Newcastle's Town Clerk, or to acknowledge the ownership of the area by Greenwich Estates. As with other N&C stations there would not have been platforms provided when it opened. In 1879/80, when a

Fourstones: In July 1966, several months before its closure, the station was well maintained. The waiting shelter on the left was constructed by the Newcastle & Carlisle Railway, while the principal building on the other platform was a later addition by the North Eastern Railway. *Gordon Biddle*

Fourstones: The original station building, sympathetically extended, has outlived its replacement. Today it is in residential use, as seen in August 2001. *Alan Young*

new station was constructed a little to the east, an N&C waiting shed on the south platform was retained. The new building on the north platform was of the NER's favoured single-storey twin-pavilion layout, built of local stone, with bay windows on each pavilion. Fourstones was a truly delightful country station, where in summer passengers could enjoy the sight and fragrance of the climbing roses that adorned the platform fences.

Fourstones was among the 2,128 stations recommended for closure by Beeching in 1963. It duly closed to goods traffic on 26 April 1965 and to passengers on 2 January 1967. The platforms and buildings survived for several years before demolition, but the original house

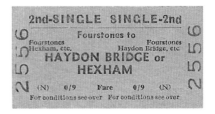

remains in residential use.

Interest in Fourstones has been revived as it is the setting for *The Station*, a show presented by the Bristol-based Idle Dream Theatre Company, written by Malcolm Hamilton, directed by Nick Young and produced by Katie Dunn.

Fourstones: A flyer for the show *The Station*, which is based on Fourstones. The imposing classical architecture of the station building is purely artistic licence! *Malcolm Hamilton*

CROFT SPA (1841)

Date opened	31 March 1841
Location	On the north side of Hurworth Road
Company on opening	Great North of England Railway
Date closed to passengers	3 March 1969
Date closed completely	3 March 1969
Company on closing	British Rail (Eastern Region)
Present state	Demolished. Traces of the down platform can be seen, and the road entrance gateposts and gate survive.
County	Durham
OS Grid Ref	NZ293099

The village of Croft-on-Tees is located on both banks of the Tees, the west side being in Yorkshire and the east in County Durham. In 1668 a sulphur spring was discovered here, and by the early 18th century its water was prized in London as a cure for various ailments. In the 19th century, encouraged by the opening of a railway station in the village, Croft gained a reputation as a 'watering place', with accommodation for visitors to the spa.

The station, at first called Croft, opened with the GNE line between York and Darlington on 31 March 1841, to serve Croft and Hurworth-on-Tees. Croft had been served intermittently since September 1833 by a branch of the Stockton & Darlington Railway; its terminus was a short distance west of the station that replaced it in 1841. Croft (S&D) continued to serve as a goods station known as Croft Depot until it closed on 27 March 1964. From 1846 the new station was also served by trains on the new Richmond branch, and on 1 October 1886 it was renamed Croft Spa.

The station was in a cutting about half a mile north of the viaduct where the railway crossed the River Tees to enter Yorkshire. Its

Croft Spa: In this view, looking south along the up platform, the signal box is seen in its pre-1913 position. In other respects the structures on the station changed little until its closure. *Alan Young collection*

original building was short-lived because in 1854-55 a new one was constructed, designed to be appropriate for visitors to the spa. As first conceived, the new building would not have included a station house, leaving the station master to live in Croft Depot, but it was redesigned with his accommodation included. Bricks of differing shades were used in the two-storey building, its central gabled section standing forward of the ridge-roofed main structure, on either side of which were glazed, open verandahs. At each end of the building a single-storey pavilion with an arched window (as opposed to the others, which were rectangular) was to be constructed. Presumably both pavilions were built, but photographs show that the northern pavilion was replaced with a single-storey building under an asymmetrical ridged roof; its bricks differ from those elsewhere in the building. The east platform had an enclosed, pent-roofed timber waiting shelter. A footbridge connected the platforms at the southern end, but this was removed at an early date. By the mid-1870s there was a tall brick-built signal box at the south end of the east platform, rising above the overbridge, but it closed in 1913 and was replaced with a wooden box of conventional height, also east of the tracks but south of the bridge. This second box operated

as a block post until 1928 and as a ground frame until 1959, when it closed; it was demolished in 1968. A ramp led down from Hurworth Road to the east platform, and an access road served the front of the main building. In the 1950s the gas lamps on the platform received British Railways totem signs, and these lamps and totems remained until the station closed.

Croft Spa station was well used. In 1911 its 60,966 tickets issued greatly exceeded the figures for neighbouring stations, apart from Darlington Bank Top and North Road. However, trains did not call frequently at Croft Spa. The summer 1896 service amounted to four weekday trains each way on the main line (only two on Sundays) with six to Richmond, and eight on the Richmond to Darlington service on weekdays (and, again, two each way on Sundays). The summer 1920 timetable shows

Croft Spa: Relatively few stations in the North Eastern Region of British Railways received totem name signs. This one features the black-edged lettering found only on North Eastern totems. *Richard Furness images*

Opposite **Croft Spa:** In the mid-1960s a diesel multiple unit bound for Richmond calls at the station. *Maurice Burns*

Above **Croft Spa:** In July 1973 the derelict station building is observed from a passing train. *Alan Young*

that the service had scarcely altered. However, by the winter of 1937 the main-line service had been reduced to two up trains on all days, and three down (but none on Sundays). In the summer of 1955 the only service was one up train on weekdays. However, the Richmond branch service was maintained, and by 1955 there were about ten trains each way on weekdays, with six on Sundays, which stopped at Croft Spa. On 5 June 1958 three of the minor stations between Darlington and York closed, followed by five more on 15 September of that year, and on that date the 'local' train service was withdrawn; thereafter only Richmond branch trains served Croft Spa. In 1967 the station booked 12,071 passengers (Richmond's figure was 43,343) and the weekday frequency of trains had changed little from 1955, though trains no longer called on Sundays. Despite the respectable passenger figures, including military personnel travelling to and from Catterick Garrison, the train service ended on 3 March 1969, and Croft Spa closed with the four Richmond branch stations. The line was abandoned from Catterick Bridge to Richmond, but goods traffic continued on the remaining section of the branch until 9 February 1970. As noted earlier, goods traffic at Croft Depot had ceased in 1964. Croft Spa's platforms and the east-side waiting shelter were soon demolished, but the station building survived in a derelict state until its demolition in the mid-1970s.

GREATHAM (1841)

Date opened	By 6 September 1841
Location	Immediately north-east of level crossing on Marsh House Lane, off Station Road.
Company on opening	Stockton & Darlington Railway
Date closed to passengers	25 November 1991
Date closed completely	25 November 1991
Company on closing	British Rail (Eastern Region)
Present state	Platforms remain
County	Durham (now Borough of Hartlepool Unitary Authority)
OS Grid Ref	NZ499268

The line between Stockton and West Hartlepool opened on 10 February 1841, but there is no record of a station at Greatham until 6 September 1841, when it was mentioned in an inspection report. Bradshaw timetables first included it in January 1847. Four trains in each direction called at Greatham in May 1849, rising to 20 northbound and 21 southbound in the summer of 1896; one northbound train

Greatham: Looking south-west along the up platform, the modest building dating from the 1880s can be seen on the down platform. *Ken Hoole collection, courtesy of Ken Hoole Study Centre, Darlington*

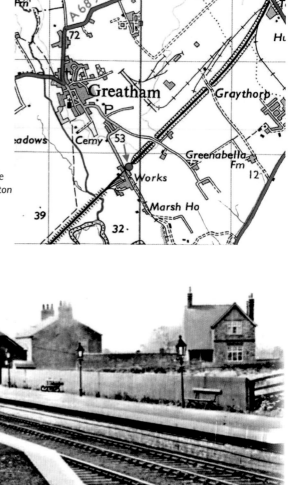

Greatham: By September 1972, when this picture was taken from a passing train, a series of gas lamps still graced the platforms, but the buildings had been demolished after the station ceased to be staffed. *Alan Young*

called only to set down 1st Class passengers. Three trains called in each direction on Sunday. By the 1930s the weekday service was between 15 and 20 trains each way, but in the British Railways era the standard of service declined markedly to approximately 10 each way on weekdays, with six on Sundays in the summer of 1950. Ten years later the weekday service had halved, with no southbound departures between 8.01am and 6.50pm in the summer of 1960. Diesel multiple units had been introduced on the local services in November 1955, and many of these conspicuously failed to call at Greatham and its neighbour to the north, Seaton Carew, yet in the Beeching report neither was earmarked for closure. On 7 September 1964 Greatham became unstaffed, and goods facilities were withdrawn on 5 April 1965. Seaton Carew survived a closure enquiry

several years later, but Greatham was spared this indignity.

That Greatham came through the 1960s unscathed was principally due to its proximity to the Cerebos salt works, and the timing of its train services in later years was related to the needs of the workforce. The 1969-70 timetable, for example, shows a train, on Mondays to Thursdays only, starting at Greatham at 17.08 and working to Hartlepool. The sparse service contracted further; by the summer of 1990 one northbound train called at 08.21 and there were three southbound departures. Few stations closed in the 1990s, but south-east Durham and Teesside lost three early in that decade, one of which was Greatham, on 25 November 1991.

In 1884/85 Greatham station had been rebuilt, receiving a charming single-storey building on the north-west platform. Built of red brick and embellished with string-courses of blue brick, the booking office had a single projecting gable and a half-hipped roof. Windows were of a segmental arch design, and there was a glazed open verandah. The building included a general waiting room, another for ladies, and toilets, and storehouses for coals and ashes. A large, brick-built waiting shelter stood on the opposite platform. By 1972 the unstaffed station had lost its buildings, but gas lamps still lined the platform. The salt works, which kept the station alive, became a food processing factory, but closed in 2002.

Greatham: The bleak platforms are seen in April 1977, with adequate signage but minimal lighting and shelter. *Alan Young*

HIGH SHIELDS (1842 and 1863/64)

First station opened	17 December 1842
Location	Between Rekendyke Lane, Havelock Street and Portberry Way
Company on opening	Brandling Junction Railway
Date closed to passengers	1863/64
Date closed completely	1863/64
Company on closing	North Eastern Railway
Present state	Demolished
County	Durham (now Tyne & Wear)
OS Grid Ref	NZ358662

Second station opened	1863/64
Location	Immediately north of Laygate and west of Al Azhar mosque
Company on opening	North Eastern Railway
Date closed to passengers	1 June 1981
Date closed completely	1 June 1981
Company on closing	British Rail (Eastern Region)
Present state	Demolished, and site landscaped
County	Durham (now Tyne & Wear)
OS Grid Ref	NZ359664

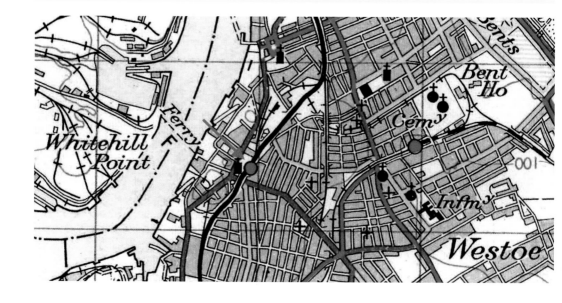

High Shields is about half a mile south of South Shields town centre. The first South Shields station opened on 16 April 1835 as the northern terminus of the Stanhope & Tyne Railway. On 19 June 1839 the Brandling Junction Railway opened the South Shields terminus of its line from Gateshead, but it was actually within High Shields. The BJR route was extended closer to the town centre on 17 December 1842, with an intermediate station known as High Shields; the original BJR terminus, now left on a short branch, closed on that date. In 1863/64 High Shields station was re-sited about 200 yards north. At this time trains from Newcastle used the route to Sunderland as far as Brockley Whins, but in 1872 they were transferred to a new line via Jarrow. North of High Shields the route was altered in 1879 to serve a new South Shields terminus, which – like High Shields – remained in use until 1981.

The second High Shields station was situated on a reverse curve above street level.

High Shields: Electric stock dating from the early 1920s was transferred from North Tyneside to the newly electrified South Shields branch in 1938. Here No E29187 leads a train of vintage stock into High Shields, bound for Newcastle, in 1954. The following year Southern Region-built stock replaced these ageing units. *Ian Davidson, Colour Rail*

Its basically unpretentious main building was of brick with a ridged roof, but the frontage was distinguished by a curious entrance, where square stone columns carried a small gable with an elaborate bargeboard. The platform elevation was dominated by a large, ridged awning, supported close to the building and towards the front by narrow columns and lavishly decorated spandrels. The other platform had an enclosed brick shelter.

High Shields's train service in the summer of 1896 consisted of 24 weekday (25 Saturday) and eight Sunday services to Newcastle, with 19 weekday and eight Sunday services to Sunderland. In the summer of 1920 there was a 20-minute-interval service for much of the day, but half-hourly on Sundays, to Newcastle, with 24 weekday and eight Sunday trains to Sunderland. In March 1938 electric trains were introduced on the Newcastle line, using cascaded 1920/22 stock from the Newcastle-Coast Circle, and new Eastleigh-built Southern Region BR stock from 1955. By 1962 passenger figures on the electrics had halved since 1938 and, on the pretext of cost-cutting, BR replaced them with diesel multiple units on 7 January 1963. High Shields's bookings fell from 301,687 in 1911 to 182,052 in 1951, and to only 44,483 in 1967, making it the least-used station between Newcastle and South Shields. From the winter of 1962 Sunday trains ceased

to call at High Shields. On 3 May 1965 the service of 25 weekday (22 Saturday) trains to Sunderland was withdrawn, and the following month the 20-minute-interval service to Newcastle was reduced to half-hourly. Further economies were effected when on 5 October 1969 all intermediate stations between Newcastle and South Shields became unstaffed. The buildings were soon vandalised, and BR demolished them at each station from Felling to High Shields in early 1972. Gas lighting at High Shields was replaced with tall vandal-proof

Above **High Shields:** In March 1957 'G5' No 67265 enters with a Sunderland-South Shields passenger train. Diesel multiple units replaced steam on this service in August 1958. *Les Turnbull*

Left **High Shields:** On a bright day in December 1962 a coal train trundles southwards through the station. *Brian Johnson*

electric lamps, and 'bus shelters' were installed. BR(NE) totem signs, fitted in about 1961, were replaced in 1973/74 with corporate identity signage.

When the decision was made to include the South Shields line in the Tyneside Metro system, a diversion using a mineral railway (the former Stanhope & Tyne) between Tyne Dock and South Shields was proposed, with a new station at Chichester. While the riverside industries and population had declined in the neighbourhood of High Shields station, Chichester was a populous residential area, and the station would provide a bus-rail interchange facility. Consequently, when the South Shields branch closed on 1 June 1981 for conversion to electrified Metro operation, the route through High Shields was abandoned, and the station did not reopen. It was soon demolished, and the embankment on which it stood was removed.

Above **High Shields:** The main building was enhanced by a generous awning carried on elaborate iron brackets. Gas lighting remained in use until the station was modernised in 1972. *Gordon Biddle*

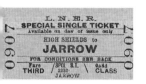

Inset **High Shields:** A totem name sign installed in the station in about 1961. *Richard Furness images*

High Shields: In its last years the station was well lit but otherwise thoroughly uninviting to passengers. This view, looking north, shows it in July 1979. *Alan Young*

LEAMSIDE (1844 and 1857)

First station opened	15 April 1844
Location	Immediately south of Station Road bridge
Company on opening	Newcastle & Darlington Junction Railway
Date closed to passengers	Probably 1 April 1857
Date closed completely	Probably 1 April 1857
Company on closing	North Eastern Railway
Present state	Demolished
County	Durham
OS Grid Ref	NZ313465

Second station opened	Probably 1 April 1857
Location	South of Station Road bridge
Company on opening	North Eastern Railway
Date closed to passengers	5 October 1953
Date closed completely	5 October 1953
Company on closing	British Railways (North Eastern Region)
Present state	Demolished
County	Durham
OS Grid Ref	NZ313464

Although Leamside, with its neighbour West Rainton, is now a large village, the area was sparsely settled when the first passenger railway service began in the locality in 1835. This was the Stanhope & Tyne Railway, built for mineral traffic but conveying passengers between Durham Turnpike (Chester-le-Street) and South Shields. There was a station on this line at Washington, some 5 miles north of Leamside. In 1840 passenger trains were introduced on the Durham Junction Railway branch from Washington to Rainton Meadows, about a mile north-east of Leamside, from which

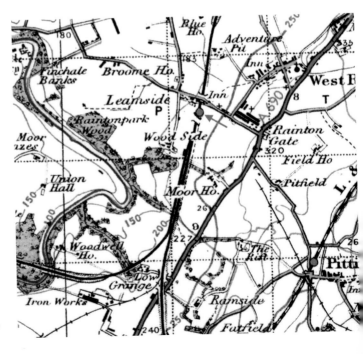

Leamside, 1947

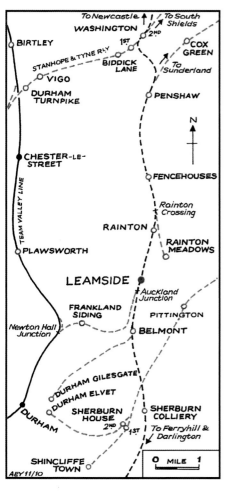

Leamside: The spacious second station was designed to allow interchange between London-Newcastle main-line trains and branch services to Durham and Sunderland. This southward view shows the disused bay platform originally provided for branch trains to and from Sunderland. *Ken Hoole collection, courtesy of Ken Hoole Study Centre, Darlington*

road coaches provided access to Durham. Leamside's first station opened on 15 April 1844, when a new line was opened to passengers by the Newcastle & Darlington Junction Railway from Rainton Crossing (a short distance north of Rainton Meadows) to Durham (Gilesgate). On the same date a route from Belmont station (a mile south of Leamside) opened to Darlington for goods traffic, and passengers were carried from 19 June 1844. This completed the link between London and the Tyne (at Gateshead) – the 'old main line'.

Leamside became a junction on 19 August 1856 when the North Eastern Railway opened a route from the station through Durham to Bishop Auckland. Passenger services were introduced on 1 April 1857, and it seems likely that the new Leamside station, a short distance south of the original, was opened on this date. Durham (Gilesgate) and Belmont stations closed on the same day. In 1853 passenger trains began to run from Penshaw (4 miles north of Leamside) to

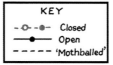

Left **Leamside:** A map of the surrounding railway network and stations, past and present. *Alan Young*

Leamside: This undated view shows a southbound passenger working entering the station. *Ken Hoole collection, courtesy of Ken Hoole Study Centre, Darlington*

Sunderland, so from April 1857 Leamside was an important station on the London-Newcastle main line where connections were made to Sunderland and Durham. The layout of the new station was designed for its role as an interchange.

Main-line trains continued to pass through Leamside until 1872 when they were transferred to the Team Valley and Drham-Ferryhill routes: the new East Coast Main Line. Leamside's importance immediately declined, and its facilities must then have appeared lavish for the diminutive settlement it served.

The original N&DJ station building was one of many designed by G. T. Andrews. It was single-storey and stone-built, with a prominent bay window, and was sited almost at rail level. It stood east of the tracks and north of the level crossing of the lane

that was to become Station Road; however, by 1856 this road was diverted over a bridge immediately north of the station. Although rendered redundant by the new station, the original one survived until at least 1959, and had been demolished by 1966.

The new station had one broad island platform flanked by the through lines, and single-track bays at each end for local services that terminated there. The modest buildings in the middle of this platform were beneath a large hipped roof extending to the edges of the through platform and supported by a series of columns. Two large water tanks sat on the roof, embellished by wooden panelling. Passengers reached the platforms by footbridges from pathways on each side of the railway. In 1912 the former North and South signal boxes were replaced with the new Leamside box, west of the lines and immediately south of the footbridge (which crossed the tracks immediately north of the platform buildings). A bridge over the southern end of the platform carried a mineral railway to Littletown

Leamside: Looking south in February 2011, nothing remains of the first or second station. Ivy is invading the 'mothballed' tracks, supplemented by fly-tipping. *Alan Young*

(Lambton) Colliery. This mine closed in 1914, and the railway was lifted by 1939.

The winter 1937-38 timetable shows that Leamside's most frequent service was on the Durham-Sunderland line, with 17 trains on Monday to Friday, 19 on Saturday, and six on Sunday to Sunderland, and 18 weekday and six Sunday trains to Durham. Northwards to Newcastle there were seven trains on Monday to Friday and 12 on Saturday, while from Newcastle there were eight Monday to Friday, nine on Saturday and one on Sunday. On the line to Ferryhill, which was to close to local passenger services on 28 July 1941, there were four weekday trains and one on Sundays, and five arrived from Ferryhill on weekdays. From 1947 the service between Newcastle and Leamside was all but extinguished, leaving only one southbound train calling there at 5.18am. In Leamside's final month of services there were nine Monday-to-Friday and ten Saturday departures to Sunderland, and eight on

weekdays in the opposite direction; one Sunday train was provided in each direction. Several trains by this time omitted stops at Leamside. Passenger bookings slumped from 61,571 in 1911 to a meagre 5,968 in 1951; in comparison Fencehouses and Penshaw, the next stations northwards, each issued more than 20,000 tickets.

Leamside closed to passenger and goods traffic on 5 October 1953, and the rails were lifted, except on the through lines. By May 1959 the platform and buildings had been demolished, and the tracks were slewed across their site. In 1991 British Rail 'mothballed' the Pelaw-Ferryhill line through Leamside. Various proposals have been made to reopen it to passengers, and although a mile of track south of Penshaw has been stolen, and track has been removed at some level crossings and at Usworth station, what remains is apparently in reasonable condition and might not have to be re-laid.

ROWLEY (1845)

Date opened	1 September 1845
Location	West of A68 (road bridge demolished). Station access lane leads to car park on Waskerley Way cycle track, which passes through the station site.
Company on opening	Stockton & Darlington Railway
Date closed to passengers	1 May 1939
Date closed completely	6 June 1966
Company on closing	Passenger services: London & North Eastern Railway Goods services: British Rail (North Eastern Region)
Present state	Demolished; site is now a picnic area.
County	Durham
OS Grid Ref	NZ003432

Cold Rowley station (renamed Rowley on 1 July 1868) was on the Stanhope & Tyne Railway, which opened in 1834 to carry limestone from quarries in upper Weardale and coal from mines in north-west Durham to the River Tyne at South Shields. The line rose from Weardale by inclined planes with winding engines at Crawley and Weatherhill. Horses worked the summit section, and traffic descended northwards using another winding engine and the self-acting Nanny Mayor's incline. The following section (through Rowley) was horse-operated, before rope-working enabled the traffic to cross the ravine of Hownes Gill. Following the bankruptcy of the S&T, the Derwent Iron Company bought the section of its line south of Consett, thereafter known as the Derwent Railway, to guarantee its supply of limestone. The company considered creating

Rowley: Not only does this superb view from the road bridge include the station buildings and sidings in their rural setting, but it also reveals the efforts of a dedicated gardener. *John Mann collection*

Rowley: The station appears busy as a passenger train enters, probably bound for Blackhill. *Ken Hoole collection, courtesy of Ken Hoole Study Centre, Darlington*

a route towards Crook and the Stockton & Darlington as an outlet for its products, but the S&D undertook construction of the line – the Weardale Extension Railway – via Tow Law and the Sunniside incline, and took over the Derwent Railway. This line opened to mineral traffic on 16 May 1845, joining the Derwent Railway at Waskerley at the summit of Nanny Mayor's incline. On 1 September 1845 a passenger service was introduced between Crook and Waskerley, where it divided to continue to Cold Rowley or Crawley (Stanhope). The service apparently ceased north and west of Waskerley on 31 October but was reinstated from 1 April 1846 until December 1846. At Waskerley a village developed alongside the railway in a bleak moorland setting.

Rowley station's facilities were primitive at first, with only a rough platform and no signals – as noted in a report following an accident on the line. It is clear from the same source that passengers were carried on the route in coaches attached to mineral trains, and that some passengers took free rides in mineral wagons. The North Eastern Railway

absorbed the S&D in 1863. Ten years later the NER improved Rowley station, whose use was increasing as it served the growing community of Castleside, about a mile to the north-west. A stately single-storey building in sandstone with a tall ridged roof was constructed on the down platform (north-west of the double track). Its broad, arched windows enlivened the platform elevation, and passengers were provided with both an enclosed waiting room and an open-fronted waiting area. The signal box was north-east of this platform. The up platform possessed a waiting shelter, and there was a siding to the south-east. Goods traffic handled at Rowley was principally ganister (stone) and livestock.

In 1896 four passenger trains in each direction, between Blackhill and Darlington, called at Rowley. The winter 1937/38 timetable shows the same frequency. NER statistics reported that in 1900 only 9,350 tickets were issued and that the station served a population of almost 1,000. By 1931 bookings had declined to 2,548, and only 753 in 1938. Together with the Lanchester Valley route, the Blackhill-Tow Law passenger service through Rowley was

Rowley: Looking north-east in 1968, the station is seen 30 years after closure to passengers and two years before the tracks were removed. The dignified, but decrepit, building on the left was soon to be dismantled with care and taken to its new home at Beamish Open Air Museum. *Roy Lambeth*

withdrawn on 1 May 1939. Goods traffic ceased between Burnhill and Tow Law, and this section of track was lifted in 1952. In the late 1950s the track through Rowley was singled. Rowley continued to handle goods traffic until 1966, and for a further three years the line through the station carried traffic from Durhills sand quarry (near Parkhead, between Waskerley and Stanhope) and the War Department siding at Burnhill. The line closed entirely on 1 May 1969 and the track was lifted in 1970.

Rowley station's building fell into disrepair, but its future was assured when it was acquired by the North of England Open Air Museum at Beamish. In 1972 it was dismantled and reconstructed at its new home. John Betjeman, Poet Laureate and

tireless campaigner to retain the best of our railway legacy, formally opened the station in the museum in July 1976. The building is now the centrepiece of a delightful North Eastern Railway exhibit, complete with goods yard, signal box and rolling stock, presented as a station of 1913.

Rowley: The former station building at Rowley, reconstructed as an exhibit at Beamish museum, is seen in April 1976. *Alan Young*

SPENNYMOOR (1845 and 1878)

First station opened	Probably November 1845
Location	On west side of Carr Street (formerly A6074)
Company on opening	Clarence Railway
Date closed to passengers	1867
Date closed completely	1 June 1878
Company on closing	North Eastern Railway
Present state	Demolished
County	Durham
OS Grid Ref	NZ255337

Second station opened	1 June 1878
Location	On east side of Carr Street (formerly A6074)
Company on opening	North Eastern Railway
Date closed to passengers	31 March 1952
Date closed completely	2 May 1966
Company on closing	Passenger services: British Railways (North Eastern Region) Goods services: British Rail (North Eastern Region)
Present state	Demolished. The embankment on which the station stood was removed to make way for a new roundabout.
County	Durham
OS Grid Ref	NZ257337

The Clarence Railway (named in honour of the Duke, later William IV) was intended to carry coal from western County Durham to the coast. Its small system of lines connected Haverton Hill, on the north bank of the Tees estuary, with the Stockton & Darlington at Sim Pasture (south-east of Shildon), and with Ferryhill and Coxhoe, and short branches led to Chilton and Byers Green. A passenger service between Byers Green and Stockton was first shown in Bradshaw in November 1845; this was a market train, with one in each direction on Saturdays. It is uncertain whether an intermediate call was made at Spennymoor, but from April 1856 Bradshaw indicated that Spennymoor was a terminus for trains from the east. In the February 1862 Bradshaw four trains were shown serving Spennymoor on weekdays, with none on Sundays, and the Byers Green market train continued to operate.

Originally the station was west of the level crossing, its building south of the line. Passenger services were discontinued in 1867. In 1875 a new station was authorised, and this was built east of the crossing, its single 172-yard platform and building again being south of the line. Four tracks passed through the station, which opened on 1 June 1878 on the reopened line to Byers Green. West of the crossing at Spennymoor the goods warehouse and sidings were constructed on the former station site. From 1 December 1885 the line was extended to Bishop Auckland. By the late 19th century Spennymoor had developed into a town of some 14,000 inhabitants.

The new station building was a standard

Above **Spennymoor:** The station had a typical NER 1870s single-storey building, seen here with the verandah in place. *W.A. C. Smith*

Above **Spennymoor:** This totem name sign was installed after closure to regular passenger services. There was lively bidding for this highly prized item of railwayana in an on-line auction in 2008. *Richard Furness images*

Right **Spennymoor:** Looking east in May 1959 the station was still in use for occasional excursion traffic, although the verandah between the two pavilions had been removed. *John Mann collection*

Spennymoor: The station remained open for goods traffic until May 1966, and this is the scene looking west along the platform in September 1967. The track has been recently lifted and, although the station buildings remained intact, doors and windows had been removed and papers from the goods office strewn all over the floor. There was even a 'Best Kept Station' certificate lying on the floor with its frame and glass broken – a sign of better times at the station. The station building was demolished in 1970. *Nick Catford*

design of its time. It was a brick-built single-storey structure with pavilions at both ends, enclosing a platform verandah; the latter had a gently sloping slate roof, with a brick dado and timber and glass above.

In 1896 on weekdays seven trains in each direction between Ferryhill and Bishop Auckland called at Spennymoor, with an additional one on Saturdays. Four more Ferryhill services commenced or terminated at Spennymoor, but with one fewer from Ferryhill on Saturdays. There were no Sunday trains. In June 1920 once again seven eastbound and westbound Ferryhill-Bishop Auckland trains served Spennymoor, but there were no short workings between Spennymoor and Ferryhill. In the winter of 1937 the frequency had been reduced to six trains each way, with one extra late train on Saturdays.

Spennymoor was the busiest station on the branch, booking 125,680 passengers in 1911 compared with Byers Green's 51,797 and Coundon's 45,586. In addition, at Spennymoor up to 250 miners travelled daily on an untimetabled service operating to and from Page Bank Colliery. This pit was reached by a 2¼-mile branch that diverged north-westwards

a short distance west of Spennymoor, and the miners' service operated from 1868, possibly until the colliery's closure in 1931. A miners' service is also recorded in 1853 serving Whitworth Park Colliery via a short branch that left the Bishop Auckland route close to the Page Bank branch.

In 1939 the passenger service west of Spennymoor was withdrawn, as buses provided a more frequent and direct journey to Bishop Auckland. By the summer of 1948 only five trains ran each way between Spennymoor and Ferryhill, reduced to one morning and one afternoon return journey in the final timetable for the winter of 1951-52. The station closed to passengers on 31 March 1952. For a further 11 years Spennymoor occasionally welcomed passenger trains; football specials and excursions to Seaton Carew and Redcar used the line, and most likely called at Spennymoor as late as 1963. British Railways (NE) was less inclined than other regions to fit enamel totem name signs at its stations, but Spennymoor is possibly unique in Britain in having such signs, and complementary nameboards, installed some years after closure; they were fitted in 1957 at the earliest, and were retained until at least 1963. Goods facilities closed on 2 May 1966 when the whole line from Coxhoe Junction (Ferryhill) to Bishop Auckland (East) was abandoned. Spennymoor station remained in situ, but increasingly vandalised, until its demolition in about 1970.

KILLINGWORTH (1847)

Date opened	1 March 1847
Location	Immediately south of level crossing on Killingworth Drive/Station Road (B1505)
Company on opening	Newcastle & Berwick Railway
Date closed to passengers	15 September 1958 (racecourse platforms 1959)
Date closed completely	7 June 1965
Company on closing	Passenger services: British Railways (North Eastern Region) Goods services: British Rail (North Eastern Region)
Present state	Demolished
County	Northumberland (now Tyne & Wear)
OS Grid Ref	NZ268709

Killingworth station was on the East Coast Main Line 6 miles north of Newcastle Central, and possessed one of the large, dignified buildings – some of which are still standing – that graced a number of stations between Newcastle and Berwick. The architect was Benjamin Green, a Newcastle man who, with his father, designed the city's Theatre Royal and Grey's Monument.

In 1844 Tyneside and London were directly linked by rail, and two years later the North British Railway pushed south from Scotland to Berwick. The Newcastle & Berwick Railway,

backed by George Hudson (the 'Railway King') with technical support from George Stephenson, obtained the Royal Assent on 21 July 1845. The N&B opened from a junction with its Newcastle-North Shields line at Heaton, through Killingworth to Morpeth on 1 March 1847; Chathill-Tweedmouth opened on 29 March, followed by Morpeth-Chathill on 1 July 1847.

Killingworth village is basically a single street, on a low hill rising above the neighbouring countryside, and it retains something of its historic, rural atmosphere. All around it the landscape has undergone enormous changes, not least in the last 50 years. Rich coal reserves lay beneath the fields, and as early as 1373 it was being extracted in the locality. In 1802 Killingworth West Moor pit opened, south-west of the village, followed by High Pit to the north-east in 1810. West Moor pit was to have a key role in the development of railways throughout the world: in 1804 George Stephenson was taken on as a brakesman, in charge of the winding engine that brought miners in and out of the shaft. His ability to repair a defective

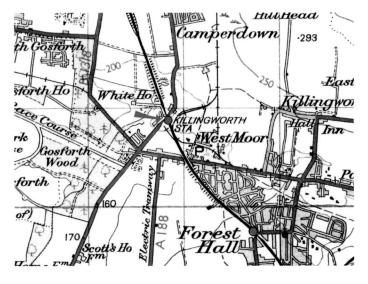

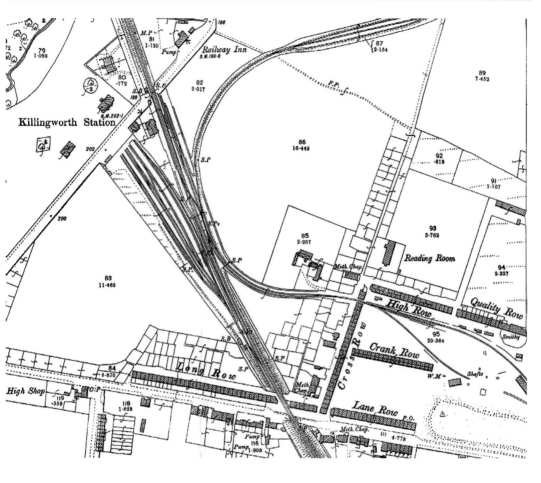

Killingworth: This 1895 map shows the racecourse sidings and platform to the west of the main-line station. The mineral line adjoining High Row served Killingworth Colliery's disused West Moor Pit.

Killingworth: A general view looking north. *Alan Young collection*

pumping engine at the High Pit impressed his employers, who promoted him to enginewright. Stephenson's energy and enterprise were unbounded, for not only did he design a miners' safety lamp (the 'Geordie' lamp from which, it is said, Tynesiders derive their nickname) but developed steam locomotive technology. His first successful design, *Blucher*, operated on the Killingworth Wagonway, and his fame grew as he undertook progressively more prestigious commissions, perhaps the most celebrated being as surveyor of the Stockton & Darlington

Railway. The engineering experience of George Stephenson and his son, Robert, enabled the S&D to use steam traction when it opened to passengers in 1825, and they were both key figures in the construction and operation of the first British inter-city line, between Manchester and Liverpool, opened in 1830. George Stephenson selected the gauge of 4ft 8½in for the lines he built; these dimensions were in use on wagonways in the North East and were eventually adopted as the 'standard gauge' throughout Britain and much of the world. In 1839 George and Robert Stephenson surveyed a route for the Newcastle to Berwick railway, which, with some modifications, opened in stages in 1847. Fittingly, Killingworth station was on this main line.

The Newcastle & Berwick Railway held itself in high esteem and was apparently in no mind to economise, so Killingworth and many other stations were built in a style that was in vogue with architects of country houses. Located close to the level crossing, the two-storey Tudor/Jacobean building, on the down (northbound) platform, was constructed of sandstone ashlar. Its projecting wings had raised gables topped with ball finials, and at platform level each wing was given a bay window. Window openings were designed with mullions, and first-floor openings at the centre of the platform frontage, and the other elevations, were also given small gables

Killingworth: Class 'D20/1' No 62396, heading southward, passes the waiting shed in September 1957. *Les Turnbull*

and finials. Two sets of quadruple chimneystacks soared above the central section of the building. A platform verandah was clasped between the wings, and a pent-roof wooden glazed verandah was added at the north end of the building. On the up platform a waiting shed with a ridged slate roof faced the main building. The sides and back were of stone, but the front – a later addition – was glazed with dado panels, some of stone, others of herringbone timber. The station was to receive a standard cast-iron NER footbridge adjacent to the level crossing. Immediately north of the crossing, on the down side, the hipped-roof signal box was tall enough for the signalman's vision not to be obstructed by the footbridge. East of the main line mineral lines diverged, one south-eastward to West Moor Pit and thence to the Killingworth Wagonway, and the other north-eastwards to Burradon Colliery, linking with a network of mineral lines.

The location of Killingworth station was not convenient for the village it served, a mile away, without a direct path or road; neither was there direct access to the West Moor colliery

Killingworth: Looking south from the station, on the right can be seen Killingworth Sidings signal box and the appropriately named George Stephenson Inn on Great Lime Road. The signal gantry controlled entry to the complex of racecourse sidings behind the camera. *David Dunn collection*

Killingworth: Brisk business at the racecourse platform in 1957, with two trains calling, one hauled by 'J39' No 64919. *Ken Potts*

cottages. When the station opened, and until the 1960s, the area north of the station was largely farmland, while to the west was Gosforth House, the late-18th-century mansion of the Brandling family, surrounded by their pleasure ground, High Gosforth Park. (The Brandling family had a significant role in railway development, principally south of the Tyne.) These features of its hinterland limited the passenger use of the station; in 1911 a comparison with its neighbouring stations showed that while Killingworth booked 34,429 passengers, Forest Hall booked 40,491 and Annitsford 49,132. However, Killingworth gained a new source of passengers when, in 1881, the Newcastle races were transferred from the city's Town Moor to (High) Gosforth Park. The NER racecourse station at Moor End (between Jesmond and South Gosforth) was abandoned, and at Killingworth sidings for racecourse traffic were added behind the down platform. Killingworth Sidings signal box controlled access to the racecourse facilities, where horseboxes were dealt with, and two platforms were built: an island and a flanking platform at the south-western edge of the sidings. On race days special trains conveyed passengers to the untimetabled 'Killingworth Sidings Platform'.

In 1882 West Moor pit closed and eventually the insalubrious rows of miners' cottages were demolished. Housing development near the station was limited, and from the 1920s frequent buses and trams to Newcastle took business away from Killingworth station. In 1951 only 1,116 passengers were booked, and by the summer of 1958 only one train called in each direction on Mondays to Fridays, with two on Saturdays and none on Sundays. On 15 September 1958 Killingworth was one of ten East Coast Main Line stations in Northumberland to close to passengers. However, occasional passenger trains continued to operate to the racecourse platform until 1959. Goods services were discontinued on 7 June 1965.

After closure to passengers the platform faces on the main line were demolished, which was common practice to prevent them from

Killingworth: The elegant station building, on the former down main-line platform, is seen from the footbridge in January 1973. The racecourse sidings were in the derelict area beyond the building. *Alan Young*

deteriorating and collapsing onto the rails, and the lamps and nameboards were removed. The buildings remained in place, but derelict, for many years. The footbridge was retained for the use of pedestrians when the crossing gates were closed, and for a long time the up-platform LNER nameboard, removed from its stanchions, was propped up under the footbridge.

In 1973 the buildings were still in place, but deteriorating, and were demolished shortly afterwards. The racecourse sidings were lifted, but their site remained a wasteland for many years. A housing development (Sharon Close) and its car park now occupy the land, and trees grow where the platforms once stood. Where the mineral lines to the collieries once ran there is a small industrial estate.

Shortly before the station closed, two small new residential estates were built in West Moor within half a mile of Killingworth station, and from 1963 Northumberland County Council developed a new town, officially known as Killingworth Township, between the station and Killingworth village. It spread across 760 acres of former mine workings, mineral lines, and farmland of indifferent quality and now provides homes for more than 15,000 people. It transformed the landscape not only by its sheer extent, but by including a lake (which was generally liked) as well as blocks of concrete, deck-access flats and the concrete Citadel shopping centre (which were generally disliked). The landscape changed again in the 1980s with the demolition of the flats and shopping centre. In spite of this surge in local population, Killingworth station has not reopened. It is some way from the centre of the new town, and bus services are plentiful, some providing access to Four Lane Ends park-and-ride station on the Tyne & Wear Metro system. Moreover, the reintroduction of local stopping trains to serve Killingworth (and possibly Forest Hall and Annitsford too) would interfere with the frequent high-speed services between Newcastle and Edinburgh. At present it seems that Killingworth will remain a 'lost station'.

On a positive note, the legacy of the Stephenson family, their family home at Dial Cottage on Great Lime Road, survives as a museum.

Killingworth: The waiting shed and remains of the up main-line platform in January 1973. *Alan Young*

TWEEDMOUTH (1847)

Date opened	29 March 1847
Location	East of railway bridge over A1167 (Northumberland Road)
Company on opening	Newcastle & Berwick Railway
Date closed to passengers	15 June 1964
Date closed completely	After 1978
Company on closing	Passenger services: British Railways (North Eastern Region) Goods services: British Rail (Eastern Region)
Present state	Demolished
County	Northumberland
OS Grid Ref	NT996519

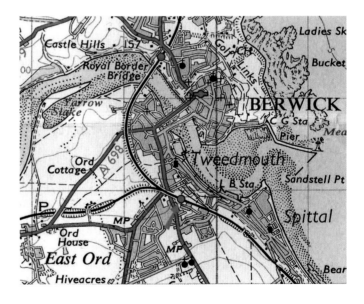

For just over three years, from March 1847, Tweedmouth was the northern terminus of what is now the East Coast Main Line. Passenger services extended beyond Tweedmouth on 27 July 1849 when the line to Sprouston opened, and the route later reached Kelso and St Boswells. On 29 August 1850 the spectacular Royal Border Bridge across the River Tweed was formally opened to passenger services by Queen Victoria, enabling trains to continue a mile north from Tweedmouth to join the North British Railway at Berwick, and completing the route from London to Edinburgh. (Goods trains had used the bridge since 20 July 1850.)

Tweedmouth was never intended to remain a terminus, and its role would be limited to serving as the junction for Kelso. Nevertheless, George Hudson marked the northern boundary of his Newcastle & Berwick Railway triumphantly with a splendid station, in a display of truculence towards the North British, which

had resisted the N&B's overtures to take it over. Temporary wooden buildings sufficed for the first year until the fine station, designed by Benjamin Green, was finished. Hudson's new station possessed a lengthy, tall single-storey structure on the down platform. The façade's centrepiece was a five-arched portico surmounted by elaborately shaped 'Dutch' gables. At the northern end a two-storey hotel and refreshment room was lavishly decorated with Dutch gables, tall chimneys, and bay windows with deep parapets. A delightful touch

Tweedmouth: A general view looking north in September 1962. *Kenneth L. Taylor, courtesy of Ken Hoole Study Centre, Darlington*

was the mixture of spherical and spiked finials on both the station and hotel. Four running lines separated the two platforms, which, until 1906, were covered by a trainshed. This had twin pitched roofs, one supported by a wall behind the up platform, the other by the main building, and both rested on columns midway between the platforms. When the trainshed was removed, glazed awnings were installed over both platforms, with end-screens provided, except at the down south end. A subway connected the slightly staggered platforms. From the station's opening, a stone-built four-road locomotive shed was located at Tweedmouth, and a 20-road shed was added in 1877-78. More than

50 engines were stabled at Tweedmouth in the 1920s, but shed 52D declined with dieselisation and closed in June 1966. The earlier shed was demolished in 1968, but the later one still survives. In addition Tweedmouth had a covered 'coaling stage', which coal trucks approached up a ramp. In 1902 the NER provided two dozen houses for railwaymen.

Tweedmouth witnessed some of Britain's fastest scheduled train services, such as 'The Flying Scotsman' and 'The Talisman'. Prestigious motive power hauled the main-line trains, notably streamlined 'A4' 'Pacifics' from 1935 until 1961 and Class 55 ('Deltic') diesels in the 1960s. Local passenger trains were steam-operated until about 1960. Thereafter diesel multiple units were used on some local services, but steam traction was retained on the Tweedmouth-Kelso-St Boswells line until 1964.

Tweedmouth: The opulent exterior of the station building. *Courtesy of Ken Hoole Study Centre, Darlington*

Above **Tweedmouth:** In this undated photograph looking south, the splendid hotel building is already derelict. *Courtesy of Ken Hoole Study Centre, Darlington*

In 1951 only 1,957 tickets were issued. By the summer of 1960 one local passenger train in each direction called at Tweedmouth on weekdays, the poorest service of any Newcastle-Berwick line station. In addition, two branch trains to and from Kelso called, reversing at Tweedmouth. The station closed in 1964 with the Kelso and St Boswells line and, regrettably, was soon demolished. In 1961, shortly before the station's demise, a new signal box with the austere, flat-roofed design of the period, replaced the old box.

Today it is difficult to imagine that a large station, locomotive shed and extensive sidings occupied the site, and that a goods branch once connected the station to Tweedmouth Dock.

On weekdays in the summer of 1950, prior to the closure of many minor stations, three trains operated each way between Newcastle and Berwick, calling at most stations. Additional 'semi-fasts' called typically at Morpeth, Alnmouth, Chathill, Belford and Beal.

Although Tweedmouth was among the largest population centres on the main line in Northumberland (approximately 4,000), Berwick eclipsed it in importance.

Above **Tweedmouth:** Northbound 'A1' 4-6-2 No 60153 *Flamboyant* uses the central track *Courtesy of Ken Hoole Study Centre, Darlington*

Right **Tweedmouth:** On 8 September 1962 'A2' No 60519 passes BR Standard 2MT No 78049, which had just run round at the loco shed on arrival from St Boswells, and drawn forward to the station. *Brian Johnson*

SEATON DELAVAL (1847)

Date opened	3 May 1847
Location	Immediately south-west of bridge under Astley Road (A192)
Company on opening	Blyth, Seghill & Percy Main Railway
Date closed to passengers	2 November 1964
Date closed completely	2 November 1964
Company on closing	British Railways (North Eastern Region)
Present state	Demolished
County	Northumberland
OS Grid Ref	NZ297758

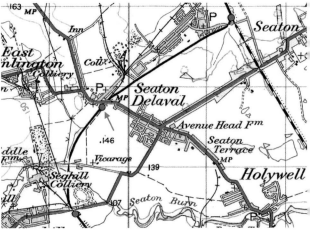

Long before there were passenger railways, coal was hauled by horses on wagonways from the numerous pits in south-east Northumberland to the coast or the River Tyne. From there it was shipped to London, where coal from the 'Great Northern Coalfield' was in great demand. As early as 1608 there was a wagonway from Bedlington, Bebside and Cowpen to the River Blyth. It is probable that about a century passed before others opened in south-east Northumberland, but by 1850 there were at least a dozen in the Blyth & Tyne area. The most significant in the history of Seaton Delaval station was the Seghill Coal Company's wagonway. This firm used the Cramlington Wagonway but grew dissatisfied with the facility. Seghill's own line to the River Tyne at Percy Main opened for coal traffic on 1 June 1840, and from 28 August 1841 passengers were conveyed in trains that were rope-hauled south of Holywell; the winding engine was situated at Prospect Hill. Stations were at Seghill, Holywell, Prospect Hill and Percy Main. In June 1844 the Newcastle & North Shields Railway began to work the passenger and goods trains. By December 1847 what had become the Blyth, Seghill & Percy Main Railway was calling itself the Blyth & Tyne.

The Seghill railway was extended on

Seaton Delaval: Looking north-east in about 1960, the overtrack building is supported by girders and the up track and platform are out of use. *Ken Groundwater collection*

3 May 1847 when passenger trains began operating to Blyth, serving Seaton Delaval Colliery, Hartley Pit, and Newsham (from 1850 or 1851) on the way. This line was primarily to take coal from pits near Blyth to the Tyne for export, since the River Blyth was relatively shallow. The May 1849 timetable showed three weekday departures from Blyth for the hour-long journey to Percy Main, three return workings, and an extra Percy Main-Seaton Delaval train. From Newsham, 1½ miles short of Blyth, the passenger line was extended in stages, reaching Bedlington in 1850, Morpeth in 1858, North Seaton in 1859, and Newbiggin in 1872. Trains through Seaton Delaval generally ran between Newcastle and Morpeth. To reach Blyth a change of trains was needed at Newsham, while at Bedlington a train could be caught to Newbiggin.

Seaton Delaval station (the 'Colliery' suffix was dropped in 1864) had two platforms. The north-west platform possessed a plain, partially rendered two-storey station house, and a separate waiting room block. Both were of brick construction with pitched roofs. A small wooden shelter stood on the up platform. The B&T became part of the North Eastern Railway in 1874, and the station was one of at least 14 on the NER to receive an overtrack building for office accommodation; at Seaton Delaval it was installed in 1885 and adjoined the road overbridge. It was of timber construction with a long range of windows, and resembled that at neighbouring Backworth. The road bridge subsided in 1940, weighed down by a wartime barricade, and for many years girders supported it, obstructing the up line, so all trains used the down platform. (This single-platform operation on an otherwise double-track line had been used from the outset on the Blyth & Tyne at the next station, Seghill, at Bedlington, and on the Blyth branch at Newsham.)

Locomotives on the B&T before absorption by the NER were generally 2-4-0 tender engines for passenger and goods, and 0-6-0s for coal trains. Various builders were used, including Robert Stephenson and Timothy Hackworth. Some engines were constructed by the B&T at Percy Main. In NER days, from 1874, freight was hauled by classes '8', '44', '59', '124', '290', and '398'. Shortly before the First World War 'G5' 0-4-4Ts, operating push-and-pull 'autocars', took over many passenger duties. From 1927 the LNER introduced single-unit Sentinel,

Cammell and Clayton steam railcars in North East England, and they operated on the former B&T lines. The unique Sentinel articulated railcar *Phenomena* spent most of its working life operating between Blyth, Monkseaton and Morpeth. From 1937 'G5' push-and-pull operations were re-introduced, and steam railcars were abandoned by 1948. In NER/LNER and post-nationalisation days Class 'J27' was the most common power for the many coal trains, although 'Q6' 0-8-0s could also be seen. 'K1' and 4MT 2-6-0 locomotives also hauled some freight in the early to mid-1960s, followed by diesel classes 17, 20 and 37, then more recently Class 56. Parcels services were often hauled by Gresley 'V1'/'V3' 2-6-2Ts, but it was not unusual for ex-works locomotives of other classes to be used on running-in turns, including 'B1' 4-6-0s. Diesel Class 24s were also used from 1961. From September 1958 passenger services to Blyth and Newbiggin were operated by diesel multiple units; however, the 5.30am parcels train from Newcastle, returning as the 7.35am from Newbiggin, remained steam-hauled.

In the 1950s many football specials could be seen, particularly for matches involving Newcastle United or Blyth Spartans. A wide variety of locomotives and coaching stock was used, including 'V2' 2-6-2s, 'A1' and 'A3' 4-6-2s, and ex-LMS 'Duchess' Class 4-6-2s.

On weekdays in 1920 there were nine northbound departures for Morpeth from Seaton Delaval, and seven to Manors North, and three each way on Sundays. (Almost all trains on the Blyth/Bedlington/Newbiggin routes terminated at Manors, continuing NER practice when they used New Bridge Street, which Manors North replaced; this reduced congestion at Newcastle Central.) The winter 1937-38 service was hourly on Monday to Saturday, and approximately every 90 minutes on Sundays. By the summer of 1950 the B&T timetable was threadbare, with few trains between weekday morning and evening peak hours. Saturday trains were more numerous, catering for shopping and leisure journeys, but Sunday trains had ceased by the summer of 1954. From January 1955 the services focused on Monkseaton, to reduce operating costs and improve connections to north Tyneside suburban coastal stations. The revised B&T timetable left Seaton Delaval with only rush-hour trains on Monday to Friday (one to

Manors in the morning, and one back in the evening), but with five to Manors and six back on Saturdays. In the September 1964 timetable the Monday-to-Friday service had improved, with two morning rush-hour services to Manors and two returns in the evening, while on Saturday there were 13 trains each way, at hourly intervals between 9.30am and 8.00pm.

Beeching earmarked the Blyth and Newbiggin lines for closure, the proposal being published on 8 November 1963. Despite objections, on 30 July 1964 the Minister of Transport consented to the withdrawal of passenger services. Seaton Delaval, with about 6,000 inhabitants, would be erased from the railway passenger map, but a Transport Users' Consultative Committee report (1964) found that the station had no regular passengers. Blyth had 74 regular users, and Ashington 54, showing limited usage of the trains considering that each had a population of about 30,000. These two towns would be among the largest in Britain to lose their trains. The 'closure culture' was enormously strong – not least among BR senior officials – and there was no inclination to improve and promote the service, practise economies such as de-staffing stations, or consider park-and-ride schemes. The final train left Blyth for Newbiggin at 11.59pm on Saturday 30 October, and official closure followed two days later. Seaton Delaval had already lost its goods service on 9 December 1963, but mineral traffic continued to run through the station, and a limited freight service exists today –

principally aluminium ingots from the Alcan smelter at Lynemouth, near Ashington.

By 1972 the elevated timber shed had gone and the road bridge was rebuilt, with two-track working restored, but the platforms and other buildings remained in place. The line is now single, and the station has been demolished.

Since closure to regular passenger services, East Coast Main Line passenger trains have occasionally been diverted over the system – the Morpeth north-east curve made this operation much simpler. However, withdrawal of main-line overnight passenger services (1988), route electrification (1991), and bi-directional signalling have reduced the need for diversions.

Almost 50 years after their withdrawal, it is hoped that passenger services on the Backworth-Newsham-Ashington section will be restored as a response to increased road congestion and long road journey times, especially in the rush hours. The South East Northumberland Rail Users Group (SENRUG) is convinced that there is strong local support for reopening. The group's first priority is to reinstate the B&T section that lost its passenger services first, from Morpeth to Bedlington; this should need minimal investment in infrastructure – new platforms at Choppington and Bedlington – and a simple extension to an existing local service from Newcastle Central to Morpeth, which is stabled in the B&T sidings at Morpeth for the time it would take to run to Bedlington and back.

Seaton Delaval: After closure in 1964 the station's overtrack building was demolished and the up line was restored to use, but the station remained largely intact, as seen in this December 1972 view. *Alan Young*

BLYTH (1847 and 1867)

First station opened	3 May 1847
Location	King Street
Company on opening	Blyth & Tyne Railway
Date closed to passengers	1 May 1867
Date closed completely	Not known
Company on closing	Blyth & Tyne Railway
Present state	Demolished
County	Northumberland
OS Grid Ref	NZ314817

Second station opened	1 May 1867; rebuilt 1894-96
Location	Station Street/Turner Street
Company on opening	Blyth & Tyne Railway
Date closed to passengers	2 November 1964
Date closed completely	21 January 1968
Company on closing	Passenger services: British Railways (North Eastern Region) Complete closure: British Rail (Eastern Region)
Present state	Demolished. Morrison's supermarket and car park occupy the site. The community hospital is built on the engine shed site.
County	Northumberland
OS Grid Ref	NZ312817

With the exceptions of the NER's East Coast Main Line and North Shields line, the Blyth & Tyne Railway operated all passenger train services in the south-east Northumberland coalfield, and was an independent company until absorbed by the NER on 7 August 1874. Blyth was developing as a port for exporting coal and was the terminus of the railway that opened through Seaton Delaval, described in the previous chapter.

The first Blyth station was adjacent to the river, on rails that led to the port, and consisted at first of a wheel-less coach on an embankment at Croft Street (later King Street). Apparently no platforms were provided, and travellers had to alight onto the permanent way. Richard Welford, in *A History of Tynemouth and Guide*

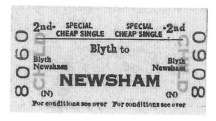

to the *Blyth and Tyne* was unimpressed by the facilities; he wrote, 'The number of passengers at Blyth would, we think, justify the erection of a more elegant structure.'

In 1867 a larger station, a few hundred yards to the west on Turner Street, replaced the original. It was rebuilt in 1894-96 as a two-track terminus with the offices and passenger facilities

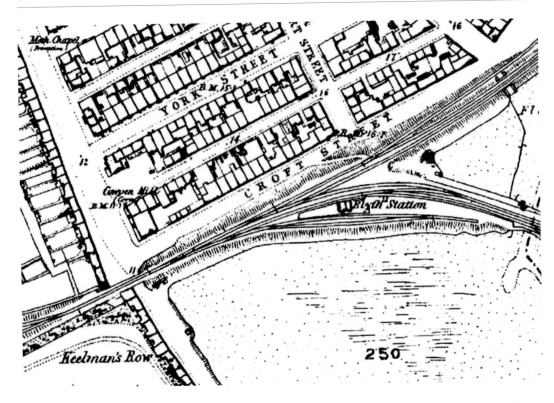

in a block transverse to the new island platform. This was an architecturally restrained single-storey building in brick. The road frontage was a long, ridge-roofed structure with segmental arch windows. The raised central section with a hipped roof for the entrance and offices was surmounted by a gable (with clock) and had a slanted glass awning. (In about 1933 the LNER

Above Blyth's first station in 1898, and *(opposite)* both station sites on a map of 1953.

moved the entrance to the right, when the booking office was moved to its left and linked with the parcels office.) Another, higher ridged roof covered the main concourse, with a third ridged section above the waiting area at the

Blyth: The restrained exterior of the station in 1963
J. C. Dean

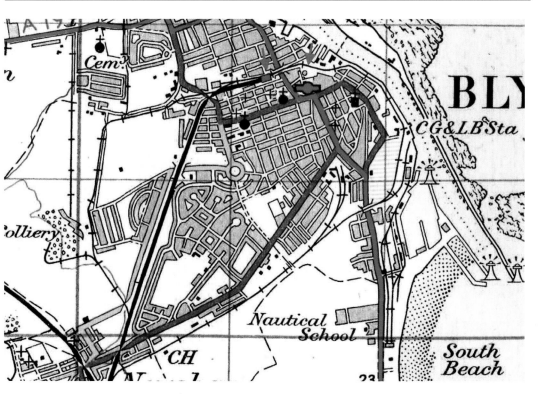

head of the platforms. A ridged canopy sheltered much of the platform. It had a glazed roof and end-screens, typical of NER 1880s-'90s practice, and was supported by austere iron columns with spandrels lacking the customary decorative infill. A standard NER wooden dividing screen originally ran the length of the canopy, cut back in LNER days but otherwise remaining in situ until demolition in 1972. In the large booking hall glazed bricks were used, dark in colour up to a black dado, and light above.

Numerous sidings flanked the running lines, with the goods facilities to the south, adjacent to Delaval Terrace. South Blyth engine shed (BR shedcode 52F) was north-west of the passenger station, complemented by a 50-foot Cowans & Sheldon turntable. The shed was built with three roads in 1879 and extended to six in 1895. A cattle dock was adjacent to Renwick Road level crossing, but this traffic had ceased by 1958, by which time the dock was used only for the annual visit of Robert Brothers circus for loading and unloading their animals, including elephants, which would then be paraded through the town en route to the circus tent. There was also a coaling stage for three locomotives, similar to those at Heaton, Darlington and West Hartlepool.

Until 1942 two signal cabins, Blyth Crossing and Blyth Station (or Blyth Junction), controlled operations within the station area. A third cabin, Blyth Staiths, originally on the retaining wall adjacent to Platform 1, was rebuilt on the opposite side of Turner Street, and controlled entry to the shipyard, gasworks and NER-built South Blyth staiths. Blyth Station box was tall and cantilevered, shoehorned into the junction between the passenger lines into the platforms and the upper level that led over Turner Street. It was struck by a parachute mine in April 1941, killing relief signaller Norfolk, and was never replaced; its role was transferred to Blyth Crossing. Some points previously controlled by the destroyed cabin, furthest away from Blyth Crossing, were operated via ground-frames released by that cabin. Blyth Crossing cabin remained in use until the complete closure of the line in 1968.

The Blyth & Tyne system's layout allowed many permutations of passenger services, and these changed over the years. Some trains from Blyth terminated at Newsham, while others travelled to Monkseaton, Manors or (reversing at Newsham) to Newbiggin or Morpeth. In the summer of 1920 Blyth had 23 weekday and seven Sunday train departures, rising to 41 on

Blyth: As seen in 1949 the station was to undergo minimal modernisation before its closure in 1964. *John Mann collection*

Monday to Friday, 40 on Saturday and 27 on Sunday in the summer of 1938. The summer 1960 timetable showed 29 Monday-Friday departures, most to Newsham for connections to Monkseaton or Newbiggin, but one operated through to Manors and nine to Monkseaton. On Saturdays there were 34 departures, 13 to Monkseaton and the remainder terminating at Newsham.

As noted for Seaton Delaval, the ex-B&T lines north of Backworth and Monkseaton – of which Blyth was part – were listed for closure by Beeching. Tickets issued at Blyth declined from 348,623 in 1911 to 61,587 in 1955. A passenger survey in 1964 identified only 74 regular users, while nearby Newsham had 174 and Newbiggin 182. The frequent buses

Blyth: On the main concourse in about 1968 the doors still carry their BR(NE) signs identifying the station master's office and the waiting and ladies' rooms. *Bob Cassell*

Right **Blyth:** About four years after closure to passengers the roofing over the island platform shows remarkably little evidence of vandalism in this view looking west in about 1968. The screen, with its ornamentation, can be seen dividing the island platform. The goods shed is in the background. *Bob Cassell*

to Newcastle and other nearby centres were used in preference to trains in an area where private motor transport was not the major competitor at that time. The provision of only one train on Monday to Friday to Newcastle (Manors) and the inconvenience at other times of changing trains at Monkseaton to reach Newcastle also deterred potential passengers. No major investment was made by BR to improve the station, which retained gas lighting and hand-painted LNER nameboards until the end; BR totem name signs were never installed. Goods services ended on 23 September 1963, and official closure to passengers and parcels traffic was on 2 November 1964. The final passenger train was the 11.59pm for Newbiggin via Newsham on Saturday 30 October, a four-car DMU that left Blyth to the valedictory sound of exploding detonators. For the next year local people implored BR (NER) management to re-introduce passenger services, but in late 1965 contractors began to remove the tracks at the station.

South Blyth shed remained in use, as did the section from Blyth Junction on the higher level route north of the station and over Turner Street, for mineral traffic onto South Blyth staiths and occasional deliveries of steel plate and other materials to the shipyard. The shipyard and staiths closed in 1966, but the shed – by then a joint steam and diesel depot – operated until April 1967. North Blyth shed, on the opposite side of the river, shared the same 52F shedcode and survived until the end of steam in the North East in September 1967, when the diesel depot opened at Cambois, a mile west of North Blyth.

Closure to all traffic took effect on 21

January 1968. The station was demolished in 1972, but the goods warehouse and South Blyth engine shed had succumbed some two years earlier. Today the only evidence of a station in Blyth town centre is the NER 1895-built station master's house, a detached L-shaped red-brick structure on Delaval Terrace.

Blyth: The station house, part of Ed Orwin's model of Blyth station. *Ed Orwin*

FALLODON (1847)

Like Killingworth, this station was on the East Coast Main Line. It was constructed close to the gates and drive of Fallodon Hall for the eminent Grey family, through whose land the railway passed. It was a complete station, with two 127-yard platforms north of the level crossing. The station house, west of the tracks, had the Tudor/Jacobean hallmarks of the Newcastle & Berwick Railway, as seen at Killingworth. Built of stone on an L-plan, it possessed ground-floor bays, one facing the platform, the other (containing the booking office) facing the level crossing, and a small verandah. An upper storey was added to the north end in 1906. On the other platform was a pent-roof stone shelter, which, like the station house, carried ball finials. A gate cabin stood south of the crossing on the down side; a siding was also located south of the crossing, east of the main tracks, but there was no goods depot.

Fallodon station was always private, used only by the Greys, their guests (many of whom were distinguished members of society) and their servants. Nevertheless, NER nameboards were installed. The favoured few could request any passenger train to call. Conditions of use permitted 'taking up and landing of passengers' as well as the handling of 'carriages and trucks

Date opened	1 July 1847
Location	North side of level crossing on lane branching off B1340 a short distance north-east of Christon Bank village
Company on opening	Newcastle & Berwick Railway
Date closed to passengers	Private station; last trains called 1934
Date closed completely	30 May 1934
Company on closing	London & North Eastern Railway
Present state	Demolished
County	Northumberland
OS Grid Ref	NU208239

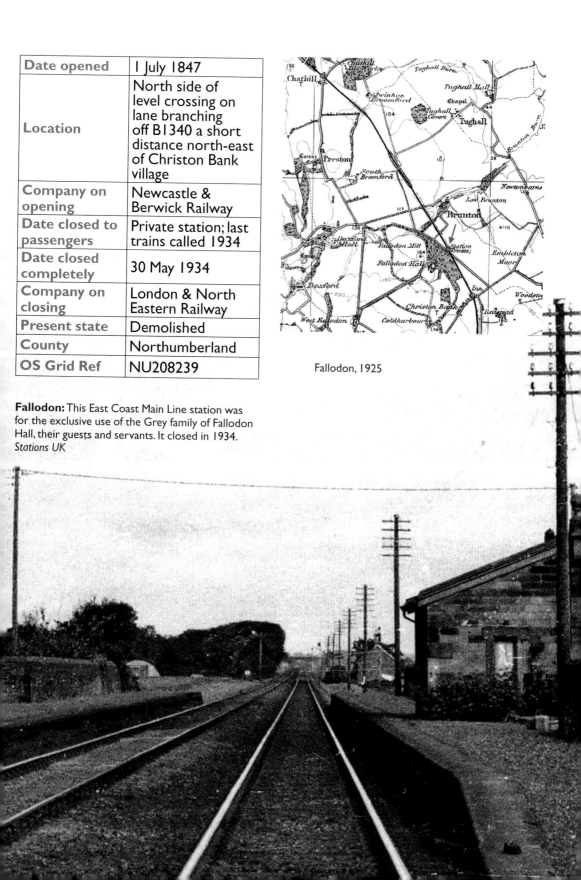

Fallodon, 1925

Fallodon: This East Coast Main Line station was for the exclusive use of the Grey family of Fallodon Hall, their guests and servants. It closed in 1934.
Stations UK

with coals and other goods', and these rights extended to heirs to the property. The station was a drain on NER finances: receipts between 1897 and 1914 amounted to £600, while the station master and porter cost £157 and £100 respectively each year. In 1914 only 18 passengers were booked.

The baronetcy of Fallodon passed to Edward Grey, who became Liberal MP for Berwick and eventually British Foreign Secretary from 1905 to 1916. He was briefly Chairman of the NER, and later of the LNER North Eastern Area Local Board. He showed restraint in exercising the right to stop trains at his private station, and faster expresses were not inconvenienced,

except in emergency. On his death in 1933 the property passed from the Greys to Captain and Mrs Graves, and the LNER wasted no time in obtaining the couple's consent to cancel their right to stop trains, in return for a 1st Class all-stations LNER pass for life. Trains ceased to call in 1934, but the station survived until about 1960. Although the buildings and platforms have been demolished, the public road north-west of the level crossing has a lay-by corresponding to the 'forecourt' of the old station building, and on the site there remains a section of wall accompanied by a modern relay room.

ETHERLEY (1847 and 1867)

First station opened	By 15 April 1847
Location	Close to New Road, just north of Witton Park village
Company on opening	Stockton & Darlington Railway
Date closed to passengers	By 16 October 1867
Date closed completely	By 16 October 1867
Company on closing	North Eastern Railway
Present state	Demolished
County	Durham
OS Grid Ref	NZ173304

Second station opened	By 16 October 1867
Location	East of junction of Main Street and Low Queen Street on edge of Witton Park village
Company on opening	North Eastern Railway
Date closed to passengers	8 March 1965
Date closed completely	1 November 1965. Reopened as Witton Park (summer only) 25 August 1991; closed again 27 September 1992
Company on closing	British Rail (North Eastern Region) (1965 closure) British Rail (Eastern Region) (1992 closure)
Present state	Station building is a private residence, but track through the station is in use.
County	Durham
OS Grid Ref	NZ175303

Durham is probably the British county that poses most problems in establishing exactly when stations opened to passengers. The main reason is that its railway network emerged from various independent lines whose primary purpose was to carry coal. Passengers might have travelled informally on top of coal trucks some time before they were officially welcomed, and even then there might be limited evidence of when this happened. As noted in the chapter on West Auckland, the ceremonial opening of the Stockton & Darlington Railway on 27 September 1825, when passenger coaches were hauled by a steam locomotive, is generally considered to mark the beginning of the passenger railway age in Britain – and the world – but even this momentous occasion illustrates the problem, since regular passenger services

Etherley: On 4 September 1957 'A8' No 69856 from Crook enters the station. A fortnight later diesel multiple units replaced steam on Crook-Darlington trains. *Les Turnbull*

Etherley: This undated view shows the distinctive building and its single platform. *Courtesy of Ken Hoole Study Centre, Darlington*

Above **Etherley:** In March 1978 the station remains substantially intact, but the platform roofing has gone. *Alan Young*

Below **Etherley:** The station reopened as Witton Park during the summers of 1991 and 1992, served on Sundays by trains between Bishop Auckland and Stanhope. This view shows the station on 1 August 1991, shortly before it reopened. *Alan Young*

Etherley: A half-flanged totem sign from the station. *Richard Furness images*

did not start until the following October, and they were horse-drawn. Conventional stations with platforms also came later, and tickets were likely to be sold at inns close to the line.

The origins of the Etherley stations illustrate the difficulty of compiling a full and accurate history. The Stockton & Darlington extended north and west of Darlington in stages. Having operated to Shildon on the ceremonial opening day, regular passenger trains reached the village in April 1826, extending to St Helens (West) Auckland in December 1833. A branch from this route enabled passengers to reach South Church (near Bishop Auckland) on 19 April 1842, then Bishop Auckland on 30 January 1843. The next extension passed through the parish of Etherley en route to Crook. Goods services on this stretch began on 8 November 1843, but no exact date has been traced for the introduction of passenger trains. Bradshaw (July 1844) shows a Thursday-only market train, but it could have started earlier. By January 1845 a full service had started, but there is no

Etherley: In this view from February 2011 the building has been subdivided into several residential units. The former station is without its platform, but the track has been cleared of vegetation, allowing trains to run once more. Conservatories now occupy the area formerly covered by the slate-roofed shelter, while the dormers and attic skylights created in the original roof, front and back, have not detracted from the dignity of the structure. *Alan Young*

evidence of a station at Etherley until 15 April 1847, when company minutes mention it, and it first appeared in a timetable in September 1847. Beyond Crook the opening of a route to passengers that eventually reached Blackhill in 1868 was equally complex.

Although both the original station and its replacement were on the edge of the village of Witton Park, they were called Etherley, the name of the parish and of a colliery adjacent to the original station. However, for some time the station was officially Etherley & Witton Park; Bradshaw deleted the suffix in 1879/80, but other evidence suggests that the change was made on 1 July 1871.

The original station was replaced with a new one about 500 yards south-east but, once again, no exact date seems to have emerged; documentary evidence shows that the old station was being considered for conversion into cottages on 16 October 1867. The new station was provided with only a single platform on the double-track line, south-west of the lines, to serve trains in both directions, a particular form of frugality that was not uncommon in North East England. However, the building was opulent, considering the mining and ironworking community it served. Its design was Gothic in character; built in red brick, it was of considerable length, and the steep ridged roof

rose from the ground-floor windows to account for more than half of the building's height. The centre of the front elevation had a pair of two-storey cross-gables, its paired windows having pointed arches; this section was the station master's house. Another pointed arch provided access through the building to the platform, where the building's elevation was even more distinctive. The two-storey cross-gables were repeated here, but were less prominent because of a remarkably steep slated roof that sheltered the platform, flanked by single-storey gabled pavilions. Venetian windows on the end-walls added yet more interest. There was no formal booking hall, only a booking office window in the entrance passage. Fawcett suggests that this economy reflected the nature of the clientele – mainly third-class passengers. A hipped-roof signal box stood at the north-west end of the platform.

In May 1849 Etherley had four northbound and five southbound departures on weekdays and one each way on Sunday. Two trains in each direction used the route north of Crook, serving Tow Law, Waskerley Park and Cold Rowley. Passengers could change at 'Junction' (later Wear Valley Junction), the station north of Etherley, to travel to or from Frosterley on the branch that later extended to Stanhope and Wearhead. In the summer of 1920 eight weekday services called at Etherley en route to Crook, some continuing to Blackhill, with the same number southbound to Darlington. There were two Sunday trains. By 1950, Wear Valley Junction having closed as an exchange station, Etherley had 11 trains each way on Monday to Friday, and 12 on Saturday, five of which were running to or from the Wearhead branch. There were no Sunday trains. Diesel multiple units replaced steam trains in September 1957, and the service frequency was increased by approximately 50% to run at hourly intervals

for much of the day. At about the same time Etherley station received BR(NE) tangerine totem signs on its gas lamps – one of the few west Durham stations to have this privilege. To the surprise and disappointment of local people the Darlington-Crook line was recommended for closure in the Beeching Report; on 11 September 1964 consent was given to withdrawal of passenger services between Bishop Auckland and Crook, and this took effect on 8 March 1965. Until the end Etherley remained a staffed station.

There were many lines adjacent to Etherley station serving the Bolckow Vaughan Vulcan Iron Works and various collieries. Beyond the station there were double-track sections to Bishop Auckland West and Wear Valley Junction. Goods trains continued to serve Etherley until 1 November 1965, but the tracks remained in place since goods services were retained on the Wearhead branch as far as Westgate-in-Weardale. From 1 July 1968 these were cut back to Eastgate cement mill, which continued to be rail-served until 17 March 1993. A summer-only Sunday passenger train service to Stanhope operated as an extension to the Darlington service beginning in the summer of 1988. The success of this service was instrumental in reopening Etherley station (renamed Witton Park) on 25 August 1991, but it closed again when the special service was discontinued on 27 September 1992.

A campaign to save the line west of Bishop Auckland, now known as the Weardale Railway, began in 1993, with the threat of closure and track removal a real possibility after the last cement train ran. Until 2004 the line was mothballed, but after Weardale Railways Limited purchased it, works trains began running in 2004 in preparation for the reopening of the first section between Stanhope and Wolsingham in July 2004. The section of line through Etherley to Bishop Auckland had been invaded by vegetation, but a band of volunteers cleared it in 2008, and in February 2010 a charter train was able to run from King's Cross to Stanhope. Regular passenger services between Bishop Auckland and Stanhope were resumed on 23 May 2010, but as yet they do not call at Etherley. The station building survives, divided into several residences, but the platform has been demolished.

SCOTSWOOD (1848)

Date opened	South platforms (Blaydon line): by May 1848 North platforms (North Wylam line): 12 July 1875
Location	Immediately south of junction of Whitfield Road and Roberts Street
Company on opening	South platforms: Newcastle & Carlisle Railway North platforms: Scotswood, Newburn & Wylam Railway & Dock Company (worked from the outset by the North Eastern Railway)
Date closed to passengers	South platforms: 3 September 1966 (service suspended) All platforms: 1 May 1967
Date closed completely	1 May 1967
Company on closing	British Rail (Eastern Region)
Present state	Demolished
County	Northumberland (now Tyne & Wear)
OS Grid Ref	NZ201638

The Newcastle-Carlisle route, which opened in stages by 1839, has been described in the Gilsland (1836) chapter. This line crossed the River Tyne at Scotswood to serve Blaydon, Ryton and Wylam. It was not until 16 June 1871 that the Scotswood, Newburn & Wylam Railway & Dock Company Bill was successfully presented to Parliament to serve settlements and industry north of the river. The dock in the company's title was not built because the Tyne was not dredged as far upstream

as Scotswood, and was too shallow. The line opened from Scotswood to Newburn, with an intermediate station at Lemington, on 12 July 1875. The remainder opened to North Wylam station on 13 May 1876, then onward across Wylam Bridge to meet the Blaydon line at West Wylam Junction in October 1876. Part of the 6½-mile route followed the course of

Scotswood: Looking west in 1959, the Blaydon line platforms are to the left and the North Wylam ones to the right. *Stations UK*

the Wylam Wagonway and passed the cottage where George Stephenson was born; the proximity of this wagonway to his childhood home undoubtedly inspired his pioneering interest in railways. At the west end of the new line, the graceful Wylam Bridge crossed the Tyne. Closely resembling Newcastle's Tyne Bridge, built 52 years later, Wylam Bridge was of wrought iron and had an 80-yard arch from which the bridge floor was suspended on vertical ties.

Despite having platforms serving different lines and – officially – different companies at first, Scotswood was treated as a single station. The northern pair on the Newburn line were added to the southern pair on the Newcastle-Blaydon line in 1875. Curving away from the original platforms, they were at a higher level, and ended some 50 yards to the east.

Scotswood: These are the Blaydon line platforms, looking west in 1951. *John Mann collection*

Scotswood: An unknown gathering at the station, possibly a church excursion, in 1918. *Disused Stations website collection*

The station house was a two-storey, stone structure, the upper storey abutting the east end ramp of the southern N&C platform. The original platform buildings (not including the station house) burned down on 17 October 1879, and temporarily tickets were issued from the signal box. By the mid-1880s new buildings, including waiting sheds, were completed, and the two sets of platforms were connected by bridge and subway. The new station building, towards the east end of the southernmost platform, was a modest brick structure with a small awning, and was accompanied by a wooden pitched-roof building. A similar wooden structure accommodated office and waiting facilities on the opposite platform. Two further, equally unimposing, wooden buildings served the northern platforms. In the vicinity sidings served South Benwell Colliery and also the ordnance factory of Armstrong Whitworth; for some years the workforce at this factory could use the untimetabled Scotswood Works Halt, between Scotswood and Elswick stations.

Scotswood was busy until the 1930s, but trams and buses drained much of its traffic. In 1895 144,462 tickets were issued, but only 17,180 in 1951. There was no visible modernisation of the station in BR days: gas lighting was retained, totem signs were never fitted, and LNER wooden running-in boards remained in place. In its later years the services on both routes were at infrequent and irregular intervals. In the summer of 1965 on Mondays

Scotswood: This unusual angle is looking from the North Wylam loop down platform towards the Blaydon platforms on 26 March 1967, after their closure. The new Scotswood road bridge (right) had opened six days earlier, replacing the suspension bridge on the left. *Brian Johnson*

to Fridays 15 westbound trains via Blaydon called at Scotswood, and 11 on Saturdays. On weekdays there were four departures for the North Wylam route. Since September 1958 no trains had called on Sundays. Scotswood closed to goods traffic on 26 April 1965.

In 1966, when the author tried to book a ticket to Scotswood at Newcastle Central, the clerk recommended catching a bus instead because they were more frequent! With such lukewarm support, even from their own staff, is it surprising that many stations failed to attract passengers? When the Blaydon route temporarily closed in September 1966, for works connected with the new Scotswood road bridge, the southern platforms ceased to be used, but the northern platforms served notionally as a 'railhead' for Blaydon. Scotswood was scheduled for closure together with neighbouring Elswick, Gilsland, Fourstones and several others on the Carlisle line in January 1967, but had a stay of execution until the Blaydon route reopened on 1 May 1967. The buildings and platforms were demolished within five years.

GATESHEAD EAST (1850) and WEST (1868)

Gateshead East

Date opened	30 August 1850
Location	South end of High Level Bridge
Company on opening	York, Newcastle & Berwick Railway
Date closed to passengers	23 November 1981
Date closed completely	23 November 1981
Company on closing	British Rail (Eastern Region)
Present state	Platforms and buildings demolished
County	Durham (now Tyne & Wear)
OS Grid Ref	NZ253635

Gateshead West

Date opened	1 December 1868
Location	South end of High Level Bridge
Company on opening	North Eastern Railway
Date closed to passengers	1 November 1965
Date closed completely	1 November 1965
Company on closing	British Rail (North Eastern Region)
Present state	Platforms remain, buildings demolished
County	Durham (now Tyne & Wear)
OS Grid Ref	NZ252635

Rivalry between Newcastle and Gateshead is long-standing and probably pre-dates Newcastle's unsuccessful attempt in the reign of Queen Elizabeth I to annexe its neighbour. In the 19th century Gateshead appeared on the railway map before Newcastle, as the Newcastle & Carlisle Railway opened its riverside terminus at Redheugh, in Gateshead, on 1 March 1837, with a ferry connection across the Tyne to a rail-less station in Newcastle. Redheugh survived as a passenger terminus after the N&C reached Newcastle, but with an intermittent service, officially closing on 30 August 1850. The Newcastle & Darlington Junction Railway opened a terminus at Oakwellgate on 5 September 1839, but it closed on 2 August 1844, and trains were diverted to Greenesfield, which had opened on 19 June 1844.

The York, Newcastle & Berwick Railway constructed a temporary bridge across the Tyne between Newcastle and Gateshead (prior to the opening of the High Level Bridge), and it is possible that the trains that crossed it from 1 November 1848 collected, or dropped off, passengers at Gateshead. The service across the High Level Bridge started on 30 August 1850, and the earlier termini at Redheugh and Greenesfield closed. Immediately south of the High Level Bridge, but on a viaduct curving tightly towards the east, an island platform was squeezed between the two tracks. This was to be Gateshead East station. Its facilities were limited to a small entrance block, probably on the east side, and were greatly inferior to the elegant building with a trainshed that Greenesfield had possessed. In 1862 a trainshed was added to provide some comfort for passengers on the elevated, windswept platform.

The North Eastern Railway was formed in 1854 by the amalgamation of several companies, including the YN&B. In 1868 the NER opened a Durham to Newcastle route to passengers via the Team Valley – goods services had begun nine months earlier – and this line approached Newcastle by the High Level Bridge. Two further platforms were added at Gateshead, on a west-to-north curve. The new platforms were generally known as Gateshead West, although the suffix was not always used, and in many respects the stations were one – for example, their ticket sales figures were compounded. On its southbound platform Gateshead West possessed a single-storey office range built of sandstone. Most of its window openings were rounded arches, but beneath two pediments there were wider segmental arches. A trainshed with a low-angled pitched roof sheltered the platforms. The other platform possessed a screen-wall with

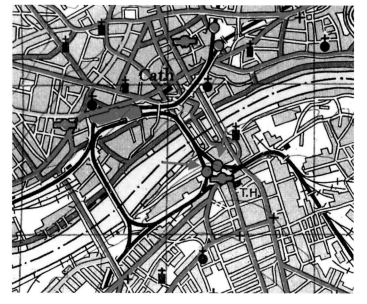

Gateshead East: The entrance led beneath the tracks to stairs up to the booking facilities on the South Shields/Sunderland-bound platform. *John Mann*

rounded-arch openings, which supported the trainshed.

In 1884-86 the NER reconstructed Gateshead East, widening the east side of the viaduct so that two generously proportioned side platforms built of timber could replace the single island, and waiting rooms and a booking office could be added to the southbound platform. The northbound platform was backed by a screen of timber and glass. A trainshed was built, its arched profile contrasting with the ridged design used on the other platforms. South of the trainshed the northbound platform, which extended many yards beyond the other, was sheltered by a canopy. At the north end the southbound platform extended further, the opposite platform being curtailed by the junction of

Gateshead East: This view is looking east in 1962, four years before the roofing was removed. The LNER (or early BR) lighting, of a style seldom found at stations in North East England, can clearly be seen. *Stations UK*

Gateshead East: In March 1957 'A8' No 69853 heads a Newcastle-Sunderland passenger train. Diesel multiple units had replaced steam on workings to Middlesbrough in November 1955, but local services to Sunderland remained steam-hauled until August 1958. *Les Turnbull*

the line through Gateshead West. Passengers entered from Wellington Street (west of the station) where, Fawcett notes, a 'suitably aggrandised façade' was provided, passed under both tracks through one of the viaduct

Gateshead West: This undated view, looking towards Newcastle, captures the scale of the station, whose raison d'être was lost when East Coast Main Line trains were diverted via the King Edward Bridge, opened in 1906. *Alan Young collection*

arches, then ascended a staircase, lit by a large semicircular window. Entry to the platform was controlled by elegant iron railings. Facing the platform, the upper storey of the building had segmental-arched windows with matching door openings. In LNER days a passimeter booking office was added. A further entrance was available between Half Moon Lane and Hills Street, and a newspaper article of 1884 refers to access from Bankwell Lane.

Gateshead East and West were clearly of much lower status than Newcastle Central, which handled inter-city traffic and was the hub of the Tyneside rail network. Despite their catchment area being limited by their riverside

position, the Gateshead stations were heavily used in the early 20th century, issuing 491,920 tickets in 1911. The train service was frequent, with more than 100 departures on weekdays from the East platforms, and more than 30 from the Gateshead West in 1896. Trains on the South Shields and Sunderland routes called at Gateshead East, while the West platforms handled services to Durham, the Blackhill line, and (from 1909-18 and 1919-26) the Dunston branch. In the late 1930s Gateshead West still had a respectable number of departures, but the first British Railways timetable (summer 1948) showed that Blackhill-line trains no longer called, and there were only two departures in each direction; meanwhile Gateshead East had some 160 departures, including a 20-minute-interval service of electric trains to and from South Shields. Gateshead West's negligible service persisted into the 1960s and, although the station was not mentioned in the Beeching

Gateshead East and West: Looking from the High Level bridge in January 1965, this is the point where the two Gateshead stations diverged – East on the left and West on the right. The contrasting styles of trainshed can be seen. *Kevin Hudspith*

Report, on 26 March 1965 BR proposed its closure. Its final appearance in public timetables was in the footnotes, the only departures being southbound at 08.34 (weekdays) and 14.28 (Saturdays only). The station quietly passed away on 1 November 1965.

Gas lighting at the Gateshead stations gave way to electricity in LNER days. The East platform lighting had brick-shaped diffusers carrying the station name (just 'Gateshead'), and until about 1962 LNER wooden running-in boards were retained, when BR installed vitreous enamel nameboards (but not totems).

Until 1966 a passenger from Newcastle towards South Shields or Sunderland was treated to a magnificent view of the Tyne from the High Level Bridge, before plunging into

the cavernous trainshed at Gateshead East. In that year (following the closure of Gateshead West) both trainsheds and the East station's platform canopy were removed, and the West station building was demolished. Gateshead East was no longer dark and forbidding, but bleak and equally uninviting. The windows on the southbound platform were blocked up, and a new breezeblock shelter and some roofing over the entrance staircase offered refuge from the elements. On 5 October 1969 the station became unstaffed. In the early 1970s tall electric lamps and BR corporate identity signage were provided. From 1 May 1972 the timetables acknowledged that there was no longer a Gateshead West, so the 'East' suffix was dropped.

On 15 November 1981 an underground Metro station opened, more conveniently placed for central Gateshead, and the former East station closed a week later. Gateshead gained the dubious status of being one of the largest towns not to have its name on a British

Above **Gateshead East and West:** By July 1969 Gateshead West was closed, and the trainsheds had been removed from both stations. This is the view towards the High Level Bridge, which opened in 1850 and links Gateshead and Newcastle with a road underneath the railway. The station offices span the roadway in the apex between Gateshead West (left) and East (right). *John Mann*

Below **Gateshead West:** In March 1972 a passenger who has alighted at Gateshead East heads along the disused West platform, past the site of the wooden office building, to the 'Way Out' via a ramp down to Hudson Street. *Alan Young*

Gateshead East: On 5 April 1980 a Sunderland-bound DMU in mixed livery calls at the station. *Alan Young*

101/A2

Biffa

| 7 | 1 | 4 | 01 | 6 | 8 | 7 |
British Transport Commission (N)
GATESHEAD (WEST)
PLATFORM TICKET 1D.
Available One Hour on Day of Issue only
Not Valid in Trains. Not Transferable
To be given up when leaving Platform
(3188)
FOR CONDITIONS SEE BACK
| 1 | 2 | 3 | 4 | 5 | 6 |

4243 4243

Gateshead East: Seen in 2008, this blocked entrance is believed to have given access to the original station of 1850. *Jonathan Clark*

Rail station, while Newcastle retained one of the principal (and architecturally finest) stations on the national network.

Gateshead East remained substantially intact until it was damaged by fire in the late 1980s, and by 1990 the platforms and track-level buildings had been demolished. The only remnant of the station is the Wellington Street entrance, used as a kebab shop. The subway to which it led forms the shop premises, with a wall at the back where the steps to the southbound platform began. The east side of the elevated railway is described by one commentator as now being 'a rather tasteful confectionery of brick and stone'. Ironically, the long-closed West platforms still survive.

FEATHERSTONE PARK (1851)

Date opened	19 July 1851
Location	On unclassified road at former level crossing, between Rowfoot and Featherstone Castle
Company on opening	Newcastle & Carlisle Railway
Date closed to passengers	3 May 1976
Date closed completely	3 May 1976
Company on closing	British Rail (Eastern Region)
Present state	The station house is occupied and not greatly changed since closure. The platform is extant within the garden.
County	Northumberland
OS Grid Ref	NY682608

Featherstone Park was on the Haltwhistle and Alston line, the last surviving passenger branch in rural North East England. Its longevity reflected the inadequacy of local roads in winter, rather than economic health – 'the creaking gate hangs longest' aptly describes a line that eventually closed in 1976.

The Newcastle-Carlisle route through Haltwhistle was virtually complete by 1838, but isolated lead mines in the Nenthead area of the upper South Tyne valley required an outlet. A railway to Alston and Nenthead received the Royal Assent in 1846, and again in a revised form in 1849. Substantial earthworks and structures were needed, and gradients of up to 1 in 56 reflected the ascent from 405 feet at Haltwhistle to 905 feet at Alston; the line never reached Nenthead. The highlight of the route was the stately viaduct at Lambley, rising 110 feet above the South Tyne. Most of the route was constructed to accommodate two tracks, although only one was laid. Construction began in 1850 from both ends. In March 1851 Haltwhistle-Featherstone Park-Shaft Hill (Coanwood) opened for goods, and for passengers in the following July. In January 1852 Alston-Lambley and the Brampton Railway opened, for goods only. When Lambley Viaduct was complete, passenger and goods services began in November 1852. Intermediate stations were Featherstone, Shaft Hill (until May 1853), Lambley and Slaggyford.

Unfortunately by the 1860s lead-mining began a rapid and continuous decline. Some cheer was brought by limited development of coal and zinc mining, but the local population dropped steadily.

In the late 1850s two weekday return passenger trains called at all stations, and by 1863 there were three. Trains took a leisurely 40 minutes in each direction. The 1910 service increased to four, with an extra Saturday evening return trip, and a journey 5 minutes faster. In the summer of 1946 Alston enjoyed eight weekday return trains, but by the summer of 1954 there were seven on Saturdays and only five on weekdays. The advertised passenger train service concealed some eccentricities: certain trains called at untimetabled locations such as Plenmeller Halt and Park Village (both between Haltwhistle and Featherstone Park) and occasionally at Burnstones and at various other points to collect or deposit passengers. Steam haulage on the branch progressively gave way to diesel multiple units from the autumn of 1959, which operated until closure, although for a short time in 1965 56-seat railbuses were trialled on the branch.

Featherstone (Park was added in 1902) served the hamlet of Rowfoot, Featherstone Castle and a colliery (two-thirds of a mile south-east) whose coal reached the Alston branch by a tramway, to be loaded into rail wagons in sidings between Featherstone Park

and Coanwood. Miners accounted for much of the passenger traffic, and 15,094 tickets were issued in 1911, almost 3,000 more than at Alston! During the First World War the station served a military camp. Afterwards, with mining finished, passenger traffic declined so greatly that the LNER downgraded the station between 1932 and 1940, with 'check-tickets' being issued and the fare paid at the destination. It was renamed Featherstone Park Halt from 1933 to 1937. The Second World War revived business, with a military camp and prisoners of war housed in the grounds of Featherstone

Right **Featherstone Park:** In about 1914, under the gaze of the signalman, some shunting operations are in progress. A motor car, with a Northumberland 'X' registration, is halted at the crossing. *Dorothy Graham collection*

Right inset **Featherstone Park:** In September 1962 a casement oil-lamp still carries the station name – with unorthodox spelling. The illegible wooden nameboard is in the background. *Alan Young*

Below **Featherstone Park:** A Metro-Cammell DMU visits the station in 1962. *Brian Johnson*

N.E.R. **FEATHERSTONE** N.E.R.
Featherstone   TO   Featherstone
HALTWHISTLE
Haltwhistle   ·   Haltwhistle
Fare 3d.   Fare 3d.
THIRD   CLASS   THIRD
Issued subject to regulations in time tables

2684   2684

Castle. In peacetime, traffic declined again. In 1951 only 4,653 tickets were issued; the busiest intermediate station had become the quietest. The solitude made it ideal for parking the Royal Train overnight when King George VI visited Tyneside. In 1954 goods traffic ceased, and the station became unstaffed.

Few stations could match the rural charm of Featherstone Park. In 1962 the station resembled a neglected farmyard; hens strolled around on the crumbling tarmac and Victorian oil lamps adorned the platform. Behind the siding stretched the disused loading dock overlooked by a grassy bank. Here, many yards from the passenger platform, was the large, lopsided and almost illegible nameboard. At the southern end of the platform were the house and hipped-roofed signal box, adjacent to the

Featherstone Park: The author in May 1966, on one of his numerous visits to the station (the anorak will be noted!). The signal box and crossing gates were soon to be removed. *Martin Young*

level crossing. Beyond the crossing, and, like the passenger facilities, on the west side of the running line, was an abandoned signal box, opposite which stood disused coal cells. The stone-built house was of two storeys. On the platform elevation were the main gable-end and a ground-floor bay window, while the main central section was flanked by a two-storey wing to the south and another of one storey to the

Featherstone Park: Looking south in April 1975, a year before closure. The 'corporate identity' nameboard was installed in the mid-1960s. *Alan Young*

north. The 86-yard platform was stone-fronted with a tarmac surface. At its southern end, in front of the house, its height was reduced and it ended vertically, with a wooden ramp added.

The first serious threat of closure to the branch was in 1959, but the NE Transport Users' Consultative Committee reported that road services could not adequately replace trains, and closure was rejected. Deep snow in

early 1963 disrupted road transport, yet trains continued between Haltwhistle and Alston, providing a life-line for remote communities. Beeching noted that closure was already under consideration, but some months later Ernest Marples, Minister of Transport, announced that the service would continue, the sole criterion being the hardship that closure would cause. Further economies were made, including the introduction of the 'one engine in steam' system, allowing Coanwood, Lambley and Alston signal boxes to close. Crossing gates at Featherstone Park and Coanwood were removed, trains

Left: **Featherstone Park:** In April 1977, almost a year after closure, the rails through the station have been lifted, but in the foreground they remain embedded in the road at the level crossing. The lamps and nameboard have been removed.
Alan Young

Below left **Featherstone Park:** In August 2000 the platform and station house are extant, and the nameboard has been reinstated.
Alan Young

giving way to road traffic. Most signals were dismantled, although some fixed Distant semaphores were retained, set at caution – one was south of Featherstone Park.

The Alston branch was excluded from the 'Basic Railway' map of 1967. The branch received a grant of £43,000 for 1969, but the Minister of Transport warned that aid could not be justified for more than two years. In November 1970 BR again proposed closure. Following TUCC deliberations, in January 1973 it was announced that services would be withdrawn, subject to an improved Haltwhistle-Alston 'all weather' road link; closure took place when the new road was ready. On the last day of service, Saturday 1 May 1976, some 5,000 passengers travelled on scheduled services, with yet more on special trains. The final train left Alston at 21.09 accompanied by a lament played by two pipers and the thunder of detonators. On 3 May 1976 rail services officially ended.

Prior to closure, the South Tynedale Railway Preservation Society approached BR to purchase and operate the line, but could not afford the asking price, and BR would not permit the society to operate trains on the branch to raise money to buy it. Track dismantling began in the winter of 1976-77. In March 1977 the STRPS had the option to buy the last 1½ miles of track, from Gilderdale to Alston, but once again the price proved too high. Demolition continued, and all rails were lifted by June 1977. Eventually the STRPS reopened the southern end of the line at 2-foot gauge from Alston to Gilderdale, then onward to Kirkhaugh, and has set its sights on reaching Slaggyford – and ultimately Haltwhistle. Perhaps one day Featherstone Park might welcome trains again.

HEATON (1851/54 and 1887)

First station opened	By 1 July 1854 (first appearance in Bradshaw) but shown on Macaulay's Railway Map of 1851
Location	Immediately north-east of Heaton Road bridge
Company on opening	York, Newcastle & Berwick Railway.
Date closed to passengers	1 April 1887
Date closed completely	1 April 1887
Company on closing	North Eastern Railway
Present state	Demolished
County	Northumberland (now Tyne & Wear)
OS Grid Ref	NZ268653

Second station opened	1 April 1887
Location	Immediately south-west of Heaton Road bridge.
Company on opening	North Eastern Railway
Date closed to passengers	11 August 1980
Date closed completely	11 August 1980
Company on closing	British Rail (Eastern Region)
Present state	Demolished shortly after closure. Line is still open, and curvature of retaining walls in cutting indicates position of two island platforms.
County	Northumberland (now Tyne & Wear)
OS Grid Ref	NZ268652

The first Heaton station was in a cutting on the double track shared by the East Coast Main line and the Newcastle & North Shields Railway. The N&NS opened on 20 June 1839, having been authorised by an Act of Parliament on 21 June 1836. The Newcastle & Berwick Railway (later York, Newcastle & Berwick) was backed by the 'Railway King', George Hudson, with technical support from George Stephenson. This ambitious company, whose scheme received the Royal Assent on 21 July 1845, absorbed the N&NS in July 1846, acquiring the route from Newcastle (Carliol Square). The North Shields line was used for about 1½ miles to Heaton Junction, where the Berwick route left the existing line. The N&B opened from Heaton to Morpeth on 1 March 1847. Further north, the Chathill-Tweedmouth section opened on 29 March 1847, followed by Morpeth-

Chathill on 1 July 1847. Passenger train services extended across the Royal Border Bridge into Berwick on 30 August 1850; on the same day Carliol Square closed, and trains were diverted to the newly opened Newcastle Central.

At Heaton there were two platforms approximately 100 yards in length. The principal building stood on the north-west platform, facing a smaller one on the opposite platform. At first the station was in a rural location, the nearest village being Byker Hill, about a quarter of a mile to the east, but in the late 19th century the residential terraces of Heaton filled the fields on both sides of the railway. The NER authorised a new station in 1861, but the first one was not replaced until 1887 when the track was quadrupled between Manors and Heaton Junction. The second station was constructed on the opposite side of Heaton Road. No

Right **Heaton:** Looking north-east in November 1956, 'D20/2' No 62375 passes the up main-line platform. The LNER nameboard, in a style believed unique to the 'Coast Circle' line, is prominent. *Les Turnbull*

Below right **Heaton:** On 31 December 1972 a DMU enters the down local platform on its way to Tynemouth, and back to Newcastle via Benton. The station retained its extensive platform roofing at this time. *Graham Larkbey*

photographs or drawings have been found of the first station, which was presumably erased by the line-widening.

The second Heaton station possessed two island platforms, approximately 210 yards in length. The north-west one (Platforms 1 and 2) served down and up main lines respectively, while the south-east one (Platforms 3 and 4) served down and up suburban ('Coast Circle') trains. The outer down line swerved around Platform 1, imposing a speed restriction on main-line trains. Heaton was one of several stations newly built, or rebuilt, after the mid-1870s by the NER where many of the passenger facilities were in an overtrack building. At Heaton the wooden structure with its ridged roofline, containing booking and waiting facilities, extended over all four tracks about midway along the platforms. There was some decoration to the gable ends, and an ornate lamp bracket was attached to the south-east entrance. Inside were General and 1st Class waiting rooms, another for 3rd Class ladies, and the booking hall. An additional 'suburban' booking office was located at the entrance to Platforms 3 and 4 on Heaton Road; tickets issued here bore the name 'Heaton EE' ('East End').

From the main building ramps descended to the platforms, which were sheltered by generous roofs. Each roof extended north-eastwards for about 90 yards from the overtrack building, and each was supported by two rows of cast-iron columns, with brackets bearing a Star of David motif. The

Heaton: The ramp from the overtrack building to Coast Circle Platforms 3 and 4 in December 1972. *Alan Young*

columns carried wrought-iron lattice girders, which acted as purlins. The roof had a skirt of slated boarding. Above the purlins was a glazed skylight raised on a shallow ventilator. In the absence of waiting rooms on the platforms there were benches protected by tall glazed screens. On the Newcastle-Carlisle line Elswick station (opened in 1889, and closed in 1967) bore strong similarities to Heaton.

The lines through Heaton were electrified in 1904, including the main line as far as Benton East and West junctions, using a third-rail system. The suburban route developed in stages into the Coast Circle service (Newcastle Central-Wallsend-Tynemouth-Whitley Bay-Benton-Newcastle Central), which began in 1917. Electric trains provided an intensive service until their replacement with diesel multiple units in 1967. Main-line express trains did not stop at Heaton, and, after the Second World War, only a limited number of 'local' services on the main line called there.

The station remained essentially unchanged until August 1974, when the platform roofing was removed, and a 'bus shelter' was installed on Platforms 3/4; no shelter was supplied on the main-line platforms. The main overtrack building survived the carnage.

LNER wooden nameboards of a design believed unique to the Coast Circle stations were installed in about 1933; these incorporated the early LNER diamond motif and survived until at least 1959. Heaton and the other Coast Circle stations via Wallsend received BR (NE) vitreous enamel nameboards (with black-edged lettering), replacing the earlier nameboards. Until 1974 LNER electric lamps with 'mint imperial' shades were suspended from the platform roofs, accompanied by LNER nameplates – BR totem signs were never installed. In the modernisation of 1974 tall electric lamps appeared, and soon after corporate identity nameboards were added and the NE nameboards were removed.

On 11 August 1980, in preparation for the extension of the Tyneside Metro light-rail system, trains between Newcastle Central and Tynemouth via Heaton were withdrawn, and the stations from Heaton to North Shields inclusive closed. Walker Gate, Wallsend, Howdon-on-Tyne, Percy Main and North Shields were reconstructed and opened on 14 November 1982 on the Metro, by which date Heaton station had been demolished. A new Metro route was constructed between Newcastle Central (underground station) and Heaton Junction, with new stations at Manors (underground), and at Byker and Chillingham Road, which made Heaton redundant.

Above **Heaton:** The North View entrance to the booking hall in the overtrack building, also seen in December 1972. *Alan Young*

Heaton: On Heaton Road the 'East End' booking office supplied tickets for Coast Circle trains using the south-east platform. Although it still carried various BR(NE) tangerine signs, it was no longer in use when seen (with station photographer Graham Larkbey) in December 1972. *Alan Young*

Left **Heaton:** A general view towards Newcastle from Heaton Road bridge in July 1973. *Alan Young*

Below **Heaton:** Demolition of the platform roofing was complete when this photograph was taken in December 1974. *Alan Young*

Bottom **Heaton:** Little time was lost in removing the station after its closure in August 1980. This is the site on 1 January 1981. *Alan Young*

L. N. E. R.
FOR CONDITIONS SEE BACK. Available for three days, including day of issue.
3809
HEATON (E.E.) to
NEWCASTLE
Fare / S \ 2½d.C
THIRD 3232 CLASS
NEWCASTLE
3809

BARNARD CASTLE (1856 and 1861)

First station opened	9 July 1856
Location	On north side of Mayfield; now part of Strathmore Court residential development
Company on opening	Darlington & Barnard Castle Railway
Date closed to passengers	1 May 1862
Date closed completely	5 April 1965
Company on closing	South Durham & Lancashire Union Railway
Present state	The front of the station building appears in original condition but other parts were altered during construction of Strathmore Court. The portico was removed in 1863 and rebuilt in the Valley Gardens, Saltburn, where it is still in place.
County	Durham
OS Grid Ref	NZ053170

Second station opened	8 August 1861
Location	On west side of Harmire Road (B6278)
Company on opening	South Durham & Lancashire Union Railway
Date closed to passengers	30 November 1964
Date closed completely	5 April 1965
Company on closing	Passenger services: British Railways (North Eastern Region) Goods services: British Rail (North Eastern Region)
Present state	Demolished. Glaxo works and car park occupies site. Station master's house survives at 57 Montalbo Road.
County	Durham
OS Grid Ref	NZ053176

Barnard Castle is a delightful market town on the east bank of the River Tees. From 1832 there were proposals to build a branch line to link the town to the Stockton & Darlington Railway, but it was not until 1854 that the Darlington & Barnard Castle Railway was authorised, and it opened on 9 July 1856. The terminus at Barnard Castle had a single platform beneath a trainshed that linked the platform buildings and the goods shed. The dignified station building in sandstone ashlar was classical in character, including an impressive portico with paired pillars supporting a pediment.

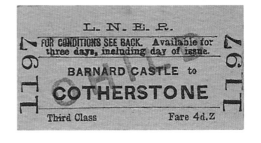

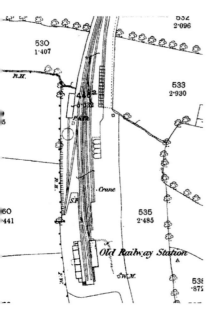

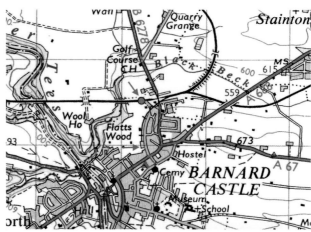

Barnard Castle: The first station to serve the town was a dignified building with classical features. Ironically, while its successor has been demolished, the earlier station survives and is in residential use. *Courtesy of Ken Hoole Study Centre, Darlington*

In 1856 the South Durham & Lancashire Union Railway proposed a line from Bishop Auckland over the bleak Stainmore Pass to Tebay (Westmorland) via Barnard Castle, principally to transport iron ore from the Furness district of Lancashire to the ironworks at Middlesbrough, but only the western section was built initially. The line received the Royal Assent in 1857 and opened on 8 August 1861 from a second terminus at Barnard Castle. To remove the need for passengers to walk between the two stations the SD&LU facility became a through station on 1 May 1862, and the original terminus closed to passengers but remained in use as a goods depot. The trainshed roof was dismantled, and the portico was dispatched to Saltburn to serve as a shelter in the Valley Gardens. On 1 August 1863 the SD&LU route to Spring Gardens Junction (Bishop Auckland) was opened to passengers, and on 12 May 1868 the Tees Valley Railway opened from Barnard Castle to Middleton-in-Teesdale.

The second station, as originally constructed, did not include the station master's accommodation, but appears to have had two single-storey gabled buildings with a waiting shelter between them. In its early days, services between Darlington and the Stainmore route used a single platform, south of the line, in the western half of the station, while Bishop Auckland trains terminated in a bay formed by recessing of the eastern half of the through platform. From 1863 the buildings were enlarged with a single through platform beneath a trainshed, and a bay at each end. The exterior of the enlarged structure featured two pairs of single-storey gables with a vestibule between them, and set back from these was a long range of buildings with a high roof and a circulating area in the centre. The trainshed was striking in its design: Biddle (1973) considers it one of the oddest arched station roofs, 'with its series of iron ribs corbelled from the walls, nearly at platform level, quaintly cruck-like in appearance'. To the east of the trainshed the

Barnard Castle: The exterior of the second station in the early 1950s. *John Mann collection*

Barnard Castle: A half-flanged totem sign. Totems from this station appear to have suffered fire damage, causing discoloration. *Richard Furness images*

building continued, its ridged roof extending into an awning, while to the west a glazed ridge-and-furrow canopy was added, supported by two rows of columns and elaborate spandrels. Although the original terminus was retained as a goods station, there were also sidings south of the Middleton bay platform.

Initially there was one signal box at Barnard Castle, but with the doubling of much of the track on the Stainmore route a second had been added by 1875. The East box controlled the level crossing immediately east of the station, access to the goods branch into the original passenger terminus, and the junction between the Bishop Auckland and Darlington lines. It also controlled entry to the two-road engine shed east of the crossing, which opened in 1865 and closed in 1937. Beyond the engine shed there was a turntable. The West Box controlled an extensive network of sidings north of the passenger platform.

In the summer of 1896 there

were six weekday passenger trains from Barnard Castle to Tebay and to Middleton-in-Teesdale, seven to Bishop Auckland, and eight to Darlington. One train ran on Sundays to Darlington. The services were not greatly changed in 1920. The summer 1952 timetable showed only three weekday trains to Penrith, two connecting at Kirkby Stephen with a service to Tebay, and one on Sundays; six trains ran to Middleton, three to Bishop Auckland (four on Saturdays), and seven to Darlington (eight on Saturdays). Four trains ran to Darlington on Sundays. This was the final summer of regular passenger services on the Tebay line, which closed in December 1952.

The west end of Barnard Castle station lost some of its character when simple roofing replaced the iron-and-glass structure in 1949. The east-end tracks were removed from the bay in 1954. By the mid-1950s enamel totem signs had been fixed to the station's gas lamps.

The Stainmore route was frequently used

Barnard Castle: A 'J21' is about to leave for Bishop Auckland. The ridge-and-furrow platform canopy was an elegant feature of the west end of the station; it was later replaced with a less elaborate structure. *John Mann collection*

Barnard Castle: This view from 1963 shows the unusual interior structure of the trainshed. *Stations UK*

Barnard Castle-Penrith route was proposed, and freight traffic began to be diverted via the Newcastle-Carlisle line. A vigorous campaign was fought to retain the Stainmore line, but to no avail, and it closed completely on 20 January 1962 from Barnard Castle (Tees Valley Junction) to Merrygill Quarry (near Kirkby Stephen). Official closure of the Barnard Castle-Bishop Auckland line to all traffic followed on 18 June 1962 (although an excursion from Sunderland to Middleton-in-Teesdale used the line on the following 6 August), leaving only the Darlington-Middleton service in operation. This amounted (in the winter of 1964) to five weekday departures to Middleton (plus an extra early-morning train on Mondays) and seven to Darlington, with an extra working on Saturdays. On 30 November 1964 Barnard Castle's final passenger line closed, though goods were handled until 5 April 1965. Track-lifting began without delay, but the buildings survived until 1971. All evidence of the second station had gone by 1976, but the station master's house and the original passenger station are still with us.

throughout the 1950s by excursions and summer Saturday holiday trains between the North East and Blackpool (via the 'closed' Tebay line). East-west freight traffic continued, although the industries served were declining. Coal and coke trains from the North East often had up to 30 wagons hauled by three locos – a double-header and a banker.

Diesel multiple units were introduced between Darlington and Penrith on 3 February 1958, and passenger numbers increased; but hopes of further modernisation were dashed when, on 2 December 1959, closure of the

Barnard Castle: On 6 August 1962 a special between Sunderland and Middleton-in-Teesdale has arrived via the line from Bishop Auckland. *Brian Johnson*

REEDSMOUTH (1861 and 1864)

First station opened	1 May 1861
Location	100 yards north of surviving (but closed) second station
Company on opening	North British Railway
Date closed to passengers	1 November 1864
Date closed completely	1 November 1864
Company on closing	North British Railway
Present state	Demolished
County	Northumberland
OS Grid Ref	NY864821

Second station opened	1 November 1864
Location	At end of unnamed approach road in Redesmouth
Company on opening	North British Railway
Date closed to passengers	15 October 1956
Date closed completely	11 November 1963
Company on closing	British Railways (North Eastern Region)
Present state	Platforms survive, and station building (minus water tank) has been converted into a two-storey house. Signal box is also in residential use. A passenger shelter is in reasonable condition, and engine shed is in agricultural use.
County	Northumberland
OS Grid Ref	NY865820

Reedsmouth was the spelling of the location when the Border Counties Railway arrived in 1861 at this remote spot where the River Rede enters the North Tyne. There were few dwellings nearby, but a railway village was created by the North British Railway Company for its employees, with a row of cottages on the

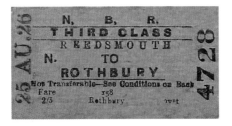

station approach and, eventually, a mission hall and a shop. The village was known as Redesmouth, but the station name retained the earlier spelling throughout its life. The NBR was a Scottish company with ambitions to spread into England, particularly to reach the prosperous coalfield and industries of Tyneside. Reedmouth's importance depended upon its junction, where passengers interchanged between Border Counties and Wansbeck valley line trains, and goods marshalling was carried out. Scottish and English train crews exchanged here, the station possessed the Border Counties' only turntable, and there was also an engine shed.

The 42-mile, single-track railway began at

Border Counties Junction, west of Hexham. It followed the North Tyne to its source at Deadwater, the scenery changing from rich pastures to wild moorland beyond Bellingham. Entering Scotland at Deadwater, the line continued for several miles to meet the 'Waverley route' at Riccarton Junction. The surrounding countryside was sparsely populated: Bellingham (1,200 inhabitants) was the largest place served. From the 1920s much of the moorland was transformed by the planting of Kielder Forest, a huge blanket of conifers.

The NBR system in Northumberland was hardly profitable, but it provided a lifeline for an isolated area. The railway staff understood the needs of the communities they served: newspapers were dropped off at lineside cottages, and the guard would convey medicine from doctor to patient. Station masters found time to tend gardens, and special trains ran to let passengers admire their handiwork.

On 31 July 1854 the Border Counties Railway, chaired by local landowner W. H. Charlton, obtained consent for a line from Hexham to Bellingham and The Belling (near Falstone). The project engineer was J. F. Tone, and William Hutchinson was contractor. The BCR opened to passengers from Hexham to Chollerford on 5 April 1858.

An extension into Scotland was approved on 11 August 1858, to meet the North British Border Union Railway at Riccarton; this Hawick-Carlisle line, part of the Edinburgh-Carlisle 'Waverley route', had itself been approved on

Reedsmouth: In this undated view, looking north, the station and the railway village are seen within the sparsely populated countryside. *John Mann collection*

21 July 1859. The BCR opened to Countess Park, about 1¾ miles south of Reedsmouth, on 1 December 1859. Countess Park closed in February 1861 when the line was extended through Bellingham to Thorneyburn; in this section Reedsmouth first appeared in Bradshaw on 1 May 1861. Trains reached Falstone on 2 September 1861 and Kielder on 1 January 1862. The line was completed to Riccarton in April 1862, goods services being introduced in June and passenger trains on 1 July 1862 to coincide with the opening of the full 'Waverley route'. In 1860 the NBR absorbed the BCR, but throughout its life the Hexham-Riccarton line continued to be called the 'Border Counties'.

Enough land was purchased for the BCR to have two tracks, and major masonry structures (except Border Counties Bridge) were built to double-track dimensions, and of excellent quality. However, a single track sufficed. The line rose from about 120 feet at Hexham to about 870 feet approaching Riccarton, with a ruling gradient of 1 in 100. The difficult terrain required numerous curves and earthworks, and several viaducts. At Reedsmouth the five-skew-arch Rede Bridge was of stone and 30 feet high; only its piers survive today.

On 8 August 1859 the Wansbeck Valley Railway obtained permission to build a line from the BCR near Bellingham to Morpeth. The NBR had an interest in this project as

Reedsmouth: BR Standard 3MT No 77011 heads south on the Border Counties line in 1953. The platform to the right was used by services on the Wansbeck valley (Scotsgap and Morpeth) line. *Colour Rail*

Reedsmouth: Two trains pass at Reedsmouth – a rare occurrence – on 13 October 1956, the final day of public services. *Alan Brown collection*

Reedsmouth: Seen from a similar viewpoint to the 1953 picture, the station building (surmounted by a water tank), waiting shelter and signal box stand derelict in December 1974. *Alan Young*

it would provide access from Scotland to Tyneside (via the Blyth & Tyne Railway) without having to use North Eastern or Newcastle & Carlisle tracks. This strategy was unnecessary after the NBR obtained running rights over the Hexham to Newcastle line, so the Border Counties settled down to a quiet life, far from being the main line that the NBR had envisaged. The Wansbeck Railway junction with the NBR, instead of facing Bellingham – for direct running to and from Scotland – was built to face south, and thus joined the NBR at Reedsmouth. The original diminutive station at Reedsmouth, with two staggered platforms, was replaced on 1 November 1864 with a station at the junction, about 100 yards south. Nothing remains of the earlier station.

The new junction station (never officially called Junction) had two platforms for the Border Counties line, and the single Wansbeck line platform (opened 1 May 1865) splayed from the southbound BCR platform. Two prominent

buildings occupied the shared platform area. A fine, hipped-roof signal box, with a stone undercroft and brick above, occupied the southern end. Placed at right angles to the tracks, it had a commanding view towards Hexham. To its north was the station building, a sturdy stone-built structure with rounded

Reedsmouth: The former engine shed is seen in August 2000. Its main occupants were 'J21s' and 'J36s', and occasionally there were six locomotives in residence. The shed closed in September 1952 when the Wansbeck valley passenger service was withdrawn. *Alan Young*

Reedsmouth: Looking south along the Wansbeck line platform in April 2009, it can be seen that the station building – shorn of its water tank and given a hipped roof – and the signal box have both been imaginatively converted for residential use. *Alan Young*

openings, surmounted by a water tank. The northbound BCR platform had a modest hipped-roof waiting shelter built of brick. An existing underpass served as the subway between the BCR platforms; the LNER later replaced this with a footbridge. Adjacent to the Wansbeck running line were four through sidings, with further sidings north of the BCR platforms serving the coal depot and engine shed. Under LNER administration Reedsmouth, and several other stations on the Northumbrian North British system, had oil lamps replaced with electric lighting, accompanied by LNER nameplates and running-in nameboards. British Railways' modest updating amounted to repainting the LNER nameboards in North Eastern tangerine livery.

In 1863 the Border Counties had four weekday and two Sunday trains in each direction, taking approximately 2 hours for the 42-mile trip. By 1870 the service had been reduced to three weekday trains. In 1910 the three weekday trains were supplemented by a Saturday working at 2.15pm (Bellingham-Hexham) and a 7.00pm (Hexham-Bellingham). A mid-afternoon return service from the Wansbeck valley worked between Bellingham and Reedsmouth. In that year passenger services on the Wansbeck route consisted of three trains each way between Reedsmouth and Scotsgap, where passengers changed trains for Morpeth or Rothbury. The Wansbeck line closed on 15 September 1952, so in its final years only

Hexham-Riccarton trains served Reedsmouth, with three trains on Mondays to Fridays, and five on Saturdays; these started or ended their journeys at Newcastle, Hexham, Kielder Forest, Riccarton or Hawick.

Motive power was at first 2-2-2 and 2-4-0 tender engines, giving way to 4-4-0s and 0-6-0s working passenger and freight respectively. In LNER days some ex-NER locomotives were allocated. A variety of engines was used, including 0-6-0s, 2-6-0s, 4-4-0s and 4-6-0s. In the closing years 'V1' and 'V3' tank engines and BR Standard 76xxx and 77xxx series operated the line. While three coaches were regularly used at first, by the 1950s one coach often sufficed. Diesel multiple units appeared latterly on special trains, including ramblers' excursions.

Goods traffic on the Border Counties was varied. There were livestock marts at Hexham, Bellingham and Scotsgap that depended upon the railway, and quarries and collieries along the line contributed mineral traffic. Road chippings, lime, pipes and timber were also carried, but the regular consignments of beer carried on goods trains gained the Border Counties its reputation as the 'Beer Line'! In the 1930s the railway conveyed seedlings from Aviemore for the planting of Kielder Forest. In the Second World War military supplies were carried to training areas.

The Border Counties undoubtedly helped the local rural economy, but there was no significant population growth in the North Tyne valley, except at Kielder, and passenger loadings were light. In 1951 eight of the line's 15 stations issued fewer than 1,000 tickets; Reedsmouth issued 4,179, and Bellingham was busiest, but still booked only 6,589. Wall issued only 138 tickets that year, many of them for one school trip. By 1930 buses were more frequent than trains between Hexham and Bellingham, completing the journey in about 50 minutes – almost the same as the train; and the buses operated on Sundays, while the trains did not. The buses served the villages themselves, rather than the inconveniently located stations, and delivered passengers to Hexham town centre, which spared them a 10-minute uphill walk from the railway station.

Reedsmouth engine shed closed on 13 September 1952. As traffic dwindled, track maintenance was neglected, and by 1955 a general speed limit of 35mph applied, but only 10mph over Border Counties Bridge near Hexham. The entire line closed to passengers on 15 October 1956. The final day of services was Saturday 13 October, when the 11.10am Newcastle-Hawick, and its return working, were designated a 'closure excursion'. The day's final

train was the Saturdays-only 9.15pm Hexham-Kielder Forest, in which passengers could return to Hexham (arriving at 12.30am) in what was normally empty stock. (The excellent BBC programme *Slow Train to Riccarton* included film of the last day's trains.)

Hexham-Riccarton goods services continued and passenger trains occasionally visited the line, the last to venture north-west of Bellingham being a ramblers' excursion on 7 September 1958; goods traffic had officially ceased several days earlier, on 1 September. Bellingham-Reedsmouth was retained for one goods train per week, reached via the Wansbeck line, and supervised by Woodburn's station master. Rails north-west of Bellingham and south of Reedsmouth were removed during 1959, and Border Counties Bridge was demolished, leaving the bases of the piers and cutwaters. The final Border Counties section closed entirely on 11 November 1963, together with Reedsmouth-Woodburn. Two days earlier, a farewell DMU tour visited Bellingham, as well as Rothbury, which closed to all traffic at the same time. In 1964 the Bellingham-Reedsmouth-Woodburn rails were lifted.

The Border Counties offers much of interest to the railway archaeologist. Most bridges, cuttings and embankments are intact, and Reedsmouth is among the many stations that are still well preserved.

Reedsmouth: The northbound Border Counties platform remains little altered in this view of April 2009. The waiting shelter, though disused, is remarkably well preserved. *Alan Young*

PLASHETTS (1862)

Date opened	1 January 1862
Location	Beneath Kielder Water
Company on opening	North British Railway
Date closed to passengers	15 October 1956
Date closed completely	1 September 1958
Company on closing	British Railways (North Eastern Region)
Present state	Demolished and submerged
County	Northumberland
OS Grid Ref	NY666902

Plashetts station was on the Border Counties Railway in the upper North Tyne valley, about 15 miles from Reedsmouth. The BCR hoped that the small Plashetts coalfield, isolated in its moorland setting, would supply profitable traffic; its owner in the 1860s was J. F. Tone, the BCR project engineer. There was no road access to the area, and the station was built at the closest point to the coal workings, with railway staff houses, a church hall, and a public house. A brickworks and coke ovens were close to the station. Two miles east a drift mine was established, reached by a steeply inclined wagonway. At the incline top, the coal company constructed a village with some 90 cottages, a school, shop and chapel, with several houses closer to the mine. For some years the mine prospered, producing domestic coal for the Scottish border towns, its workforce reaching 126 in 1914. There was still no road access to the outside world, so the communities and industries at Plashetts remained dependent upon their railway and station.

The platform of Plashetts station had a distinctive single-storey stone building with round-headed windows, adjoining a water tower, prominently mounted on a two-storey structure. A network of sidings adjacent to the running line also served installations at the foot of Plashetts Colliery incline.

Plashetts colliery closed in the General Strike of 1926. Underground conditions deteriorated, and when it reopened its workforce was fewer than 20. It closed again in 1935 and the colliery villages were abandoned. In the 1930s the moorland scenery at Plashetts was transformed by the development of Kielder

Plashetts: Looking east in about 1910, one platform served trains in both directions. As at Reedsmouth, the water tank was a prominent feature of the station. *John Alsop collection*

Plashetts: Looking south-east in December 1974, the section of the station building that supported the water tank has gone. In the distance on the extreme left the route of the steeply inclined wagonway to the former hilltop colliery and village can be seen slicing through the forest. *Alan Young*

station, Lewiefield Halt, from where they would walk to school. From 2 January 1956 the station was unstaffed. After closure to passengers in 1956 the goods facilities were retained until complete closure between Bellingham and Riccarton two years later. In 1974 the platform and building (minus water tower) remained, but they were soon demolished, as the landscape of the North Tyne valley was transformed yet again, this time by the creation of Kielder Water – which has obliterated the station site.

Forest. The ruins of the colliery villages, surrounded by Sitka Spruce forest, were demolished by the Forestry Commission in 1952.

By the 1950s goods traffic at Plashetts station was minimal, and many of the sidings and the signal box had been removed. Passenger traffic dwindled too as most of the homes and industry once served by the station had gone; however, the train was still handy for primary school children in Plashetts who travelled to the next

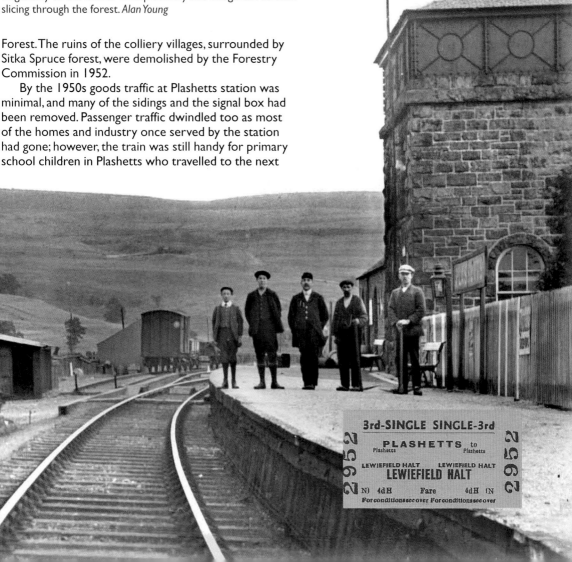

WITTON GILBERT (1862)

Date opened	1 September 1862
Location	On west side of track leading south from Wallnook Lane in Langley Park village
Company on opening	North Eastern Railway
Date closed to passengers	1 May 1939
Date closed completely	30 September 1963
Company on closing	Passenger services: London & North Eastern Railway Goods services: British Railways (North Eastern Region)
Present state	Eastbound platform survives, and station building is a private residence.
County	Durham
OS Grid Ref	NZ219453

Although the station is adjacent to the former mining village of Langley Park, it takes its name from the long-established

village about a mile to the east. The pit at Langley Park opened in 1875, and its village grew rapidly, housing some 5,000 people by 1911. The railway was built principally to serve the ironworks established at Consett in 1841, which could not be sustained by local ores and required improved access to the supplies in the Cleveland Hills in the North Riding of Yorkshire and to the rapidly expanding iron-working town of Middlesbrough. Inconvenient, circuitous rail links existed between the two towns, so a direct route through the valley of the River Browney was selected for the NER's 12¼-mile Lanchester Valley branch from Relly Mill Junction near Durham, and it received the Royal Assent on 13 July 1857. Construction began in February 1861, the delay being related to the financial straits of the Consett ironworks. Engineering work

Witton Gilbert: In this early 20th century view of the station building, the architectural features of coursed, rock-faced sandstone and crow-stepped gables can clearly be seen. *Disused Stations website collection*

Right **Witton Gilbert:** Again in the early 20th century passengers throng the up platform, presumably awaiting an excursion train. *Courtesy of Ken Hoole Study Centre, Darlington*

Below right **Witton Gilbert:** By March 1978 the station building was in residential use, as it still is. The signal box has been altered, with new windows (one of which appears to have been smashed), but it retains its nameplate. *Alan Young*

Bottom **Witton Gilbert:** The station building, in residential use, is seen in February 2011. *Alan Young*

included a number of bridges spanning the River Browney and a 235-yard viaduct east of Knitsley, built mainly of wood. By 1915 the viaduct was in need of major repairs, but instead it was encased in an embankment formed of colliery slag and old ballast. The line opened on 1 September 1862. In 1870 Lord Lambton, who owned land in the valley, accepted an application to prospect for coal, and the following year reserves were found. The NER doubled the track eastward from a point just north-west of Lanchester in anticipation of colliery demand, and mines soon opened along the line. Witton Gilbert received a second platform; it was staggered to the east of the original and was provided with a waiting shed.

The four original branch stations at Consett, Knitsley, Lanchester and Witton Gilbert received attractive buildings in rock-faced stone, in a style also found on the Grosmont-Pickering/Castleton and Pateley Bridge lines. These were made distinctive by crow-stepped gables, a feature associated with Scottish architecture, at the ends of the main two-storey house and the

single-storey extensions. A centrally placed single-storey bay window faced the platform, and a two-storey extension, lacking the gable embellishment, was added on the opposite side of the building.

In 1863 there were three passenger trains each way, on weekdays only, between Durham and Consett. By 1886 the frequency had increased to five each way, and six on Saturdays (by which time Benfieldside, later known as Blackhill, had replaced the first Consett station). Regular Sunday trains were introduced in 1899. Into the 1920s the service frequency had not changed greatly, but by the winter of 1937-38 there were only four weekday trains to Blackhill, and three extras later on Saturdays, with five to Durham on weekdays and six on Saturdays; Sunday services had ceased by that time.

Goods traffic handled at Witton Gilbert just before the First World War was principally creosote, tar and pitch, scrap iron and steel and manure. The goods shed was south of the through tracks, facing the main building.

Despite the development of collieries in the valley, much of the catchment area of the station remained rural. In 1900 the station booked 47,096 passengers, declining to 41,610 in 1911. In his returns for 1928 the station master noted that 'passenger traffic is adversely affected by increased bus services here to Newcastle, Chester-le-Street, South Shields, Consett and Durham etc'. His colleague at Lanchester opined that 'the decrease in passenger traffic [is] owing to poor and inadequate train service and road competition'. Witton Gilbert issued only 15,086 tickets in 1932. In that year a total of 33,151 passengers were booked at the Lanchester valley stations, falling to 15,303 in 1938.

The Durham-Blackhill line was an early closure, with the last passenger trains running in 1939. The stations were occasionally used by Miners' Gala excursion trains after that date, the last recorded being on 17 July 1954. Goods traffic continued until 1965 when Lanchester station was the last on the line to lose its service. The branch closed entirely in 1966, when minerals were diverted to road transport. Consett steelworks rail traffic was re-routed via Annfield Plain and South Pelaw at this time. The track was lifted in 1967.

The line has now been converted into The Lanchester Valley Railway Path and Cycle Way running from Lydgetts Junction just south of Consett to the Broompark Picnic Area near Stonebridge. Witton Gilbert's station building is in residential use, with its adjacent platform area turned into a garden.

WOODBURN (1865)

Date opened	1 May 1865
Location	Immediately east of former railway bridge under A68 about ½ mile south-east of West Woodburn village
Company on opening	North British Railway
Date closed to passengers	15 September 1952
Date closed completely	3 October 1966
Company on closing	Passenger services: British Railways (North Eastern Region) Goods services: British Rail (North Eastern Region)
Present state	Former station building is beautifully maintained in residential use, with trackbed and platform incorporated into garden.
County	Northumberland
OS Grid Ref	NY899861

We have already savoured the delights of Reedsmouth and Plashetts on the Border Counties Railway – the line partly financed, then operated, by the North British Railway, a Scottish company intent on having its own route to Tyneside. The BCR provided access to Hexham – on the Newcastle & Carlisle Railway – but an opportunity to operate all the way to Newcastle opened up thanks to the Wansbeck Valley Railway scheme. This was essentially a local project for a line from Bellingham in the North Tyne valley to Morpeth, intended to stimulate agriculture and mining in rather remote, inaccessible countryside, but significantly the NBR Chairman was a member of the WVR board. His strategy was to link the new line (to be operated by the NBR) with the independent Blyth & Tyne Railway system at Morpeth, thereby giving the NBR access to the Northumberland coalfield, the port of Blyth and Tyneside without using North Eastern Railway lines. The WVR gained parliamentary approval on 8 August 1859 for the 25¼-mile railway.

J. F. Tone, who had also worked on the BCR and B&T, was appointed engineer, and in 1861 construction of the WVR started from the Morpeth end. Bridges were built to accommodate double track, but earthworks were only to single-track dimensions, and as it turned out only a single line was required. Before the line was complete, in 1863 the NER absorbed the Newcastle & Carlisle Railway, and an agreement was reached to allow NBR trains access to Newcastle from Hexham. The Wansbeck Valley route therefore lost any strategic importance. It had opened to passengers from Morpeth to Scotsgap on 23

Woodburn: On 9 November 1963 the RCTS/SLS 'Wansbeck Wanderer' rail tour headed by 2-6-0 No 43129 visited the station. At this time it was open only to goods services and occasional troop trains. Two days later the line from here to Bellingham, via Reedsmouth, closed to all traffic. *Brian Johnson*

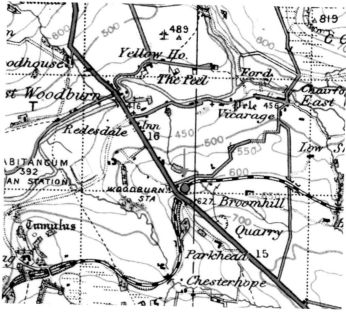

July 1862, using NBR locomotives and stock, extending to Knowesgate in October 1863. The NBR having absorbed the Wansbeck Railway (as it had been renamed) could have abandoned the 10 miles from Knowesgate to Bellingham,

Left **Woodburn:** 'J27' No 65842 draws a lightly loaded goods train into Woodburn in September 1966. *J. M. Boyes, Colour Rail*

Below **Woodburn:** LM 4MT No 43000 was one of the pair of locomotives that headed the Gosforth Round Table's 'Wansbeck Piper' on 2 October 1966, the final passenger train to Woodburn. The engine is seen on the short section of track that remained south of the station. *Alan Young*

Opposite top **Woodburn:** Two travelling companions have scaled the tall NBR signal post immediately south of the station on 2 October 1966. The view of No 43000 was taken from this vantage point. *Alan Young*

but it expected some revenue from local farms, mines and the limited population, and pressed on through Woodburn to the North Tyne valley. Acknowledging that traffic on the Wansbeck line would be to and from Hexham, rather than Scotland, the junction with the Border Counties at Reedsmouth was altered to face south instead of north.

From Morpeth the railway – affectionately known as the 'Wanny' – meandered through undulating farmland to Scotsgap, climbing for long stretches at 1 in 67½ after Angerton. Beyond Scotsgap the climb continued over the moors to Knowesgate, mostly at 1 in 70/71. The *Newcastle Chronicle* report of the opening (1865) noted that 'after passing Knowe's Gate the country assumes a bolder character, heath-covered hills, with numerous boulders peeping through the purple mantle ... sheep and black cattle dot the landscape, the latter, unacquainted apparently with the wonders of steam, scampering wildly off on the approach of the train.' After rising to nearly 850 feet at Summit Cottages, a 3-mile 1 in 62 descent led to Woodburn. The falling gradient continued to Reedsmouth. The line tended to follow the contours to reduce engineering expense, and no tunnels or viaducts were required. The curvature and gradients ensured that trains made leisurely progress along the line.

In 1863 three weekday and two Sunday trains plied between Morpeth and Scotsgap, a 35-minute journey, extending to Knowesgate and Reedsmouth (without a Sunday service) when they opened. Scotsgap became the junction in 1870 for Rothbury. Within a

few years Morpeth-Rothbury trains were introduced, relegating the line through Woodburn to branch-line status. Three Scotsgap-Reedsmouth trains each way (four on Tuesdays, Hexham's market day) continued until the Second World War began; thereafter only two ran. In the 1930s scenic circular tours visited the line. With the development of Otterburn and Redesdale military training areas after the First World War, troop trains provided an increasing proportion of traffic on the 'Wanny', and freight traffic, including military stores and artillery, was handled at Knowesgate and Woodburn. Locomotives used on the line were NBR Class 'R' (LNER 'D51'), 'D' ('J33'), and 'C' ('J36') by 1900, and 'G5' and 'J21' in LNER/BR days, based at Rothbury.

Passenger traffic was always light, one coach sufficing for most services. In 1880 Woodburn issued only 7,508 tickets, and nearby Knowesgate 4,507; by 1951 Woodburn was the busiest station between Morpeth and Reedsmouth, with 1,108 bookings, while Knowesgate was the quietest with 237 – equivalent to fewer than five passengers per week. Passenger trains were withdrawn on 15 September 1952, and replacement buses were provided by Messrs Batty (Morpeth-Scotsgap-Cambo) and Tait (Morpeth-Knowegate-Kirkwhelpington). Goods trains ceased to operate west of Woodburn and on the Rothbury branch in 1963. The Broomhope branch, joining the 'Wanny' between Woodburn and Reedsmouth, closed at the same time; Broomhope quarry had been abandoned in 1879, but it was acquired for weapons testing by the Newcastle-based Armstrong armaments factory, long before the nearby military ranges were established, and until 1963 the branch continued in use for weaponry trains. Military traffic (goods and passenger) remained the life-blood of the Morpeth-Woodburn line until it closed in 1966; Blyth-based 'J27' 0-6-0s and Class 25 diesels hauled these trains.

Woodburn station served West Woodburn village, about half a mile north, Otterburn, and scattered farms. The single

platform was on the north-west side of the running line. A parallel siding for mineral traffic was extended into a loop by 1895, and a signal box was built about 1890. Sidings and a goods platform were north-east of the passenger facilities. The station building was a plain, single-storey structure built of stone with a wood-and-glass-fronted booking/waiting area. Unusually for such a remote location. the

Woodburn: In December 1974, eight years after complete closure, the platform and station building show little alteration; even the electric lamps remain in place. The goods sidings are in use as a coal merchant's yard. *Alan Young*

station had electric lighting. In its later years military traffic associated with the Otterburn artillery ranges kept the station in business, but it occasionally hosted excursions. Until complete closure at least one LNER nameplate remained on the building.

From about 1893 until 1906 Woodburn station yard was the southern terminus of a 14-mile 3-foot-gauge contractor's railway to Catcleugh, where a reservoir dam was under construction, and on which there was an informal passenger train service using open trucks and four-wheel coaches. Passengers on the Catcleugh line had to join and leave trains 500 yards short of Woodburn station, because of a dangerously steep gradient on this section.

In the mid-1960s Gosforth Round Table took a lively interest in the surviving Woodburn branch, dubbing it the Heatherbell Line, 'England's northernmost, Scottishmost, forgottenmost branch line that no-one remembered to close'. The group chartered diesel multiple units for the 'Bellingham Belle' (19 September 1964, repeated a year later), and the 'Wood Burner' (1 July 1966). Foot and mouth disease thwarted plans for a September 1966 trip, but the 'Wansbeck Piper' ran on 2 October 1966, the day before complete closure. Two LM 4MT 2-6-0 engines coupled back to back hauled the 11 maroon corridor coaches. The author travelled on the 1964 'Bellingham Belle' and 1966 'Wansbeck Piper'. The latter was on a sunny autumn afternoon, and photographic stops were made at Angerton and Scotsgap, their platforms overwhelmed by many of the 645 passengers. On the moorland stretch, the sound of the engines struggling up the gradient, the smell of steam, and the sight of sunlight diffusing through it are abiding memories. At intervals photographers appeared in the heather, recording the historic moment; others in cars raced the train, seeking vantage points to view the event. Sheep on the line caused two unscheduled stops. Thirty-seven minutes at Woodburn was sufficient time to explore the remaining short section of track towards Reedsmouth, and to scale the rickety North British signal-post to view the locomotives as they ran round the train. It was a sad moment when, at 17.00, the excursion departed to the strains of a piper playing a lament, and exploding detonators. A steam-hauled demolition train soon dismantled the last length of Scottish railway in England. Much of the trackbed survives, and most station sites are well preserved, none more so than Woodburn.

Woodburn: Despite some alteration the station building retains much of its character, as seen here in April 2009, but the goods sidings in the background have been redeveloped for residential use. *Alan Young*

ROWLANDS GILL (1867)

Date opened	2 December 1867
Location	On south side of Station Road
Company on opening	North Eastern Railway
Date closed to passengers	1 February 1954
Date closed completely	11 November 1963
Company on closing	British Railways (North Eastern Region)
Present state	Edge stones from one platform and station master's house survive
County	Durham (now Tyne & Wear)
OS Grid Ref	NZ168584

The River Derwent in north-west County Durham rises in Pennine moorland and, as it flows northwards, occupies a deep, winding wooded valley, before emerging into the floodplain of the River Tyne, which it joins near Blaydon. Although the valley has a long industrial history based on coal and iron, it was never disfigured by continuous urbanisation, and the railway that served Rowlands Gill and the Derwent Valley for a little under 100 years, is now a cycle route and footpath through a tranquil landscape.

Settlements existed at intervals along the valley floor long before the railway arrived, and it is believed that coal deposits were worked near Rowlands Gill in the 14th century. At Shotley Bridge, some 6 miles up the valley from Rowlands Gill, German swordsmiths settled in the late 16th and early 17th century, attracted by the supplies of iron ore – which would, in the 19th century, give rise to the industry at Consett. A somewhat different economic asset of Shotley Bridge was its spa, which attracted many visitors in the late 19th century. The arrival of the railway stimulated mining, with Victoria Garesfield Colliery opening on higher ground, west of Rowlands Gill, in 1870, and Lily Drift, to the north, in 1877.

In July 1862 the North Eastern Railway's 'Blaydon & Conside' branch received the Royal Assent, but there was no sense of urgency in beginning its construction. Work began in 1865 and the line opened on 2 December 1867. It was steeply graded, rising from just above sea level at Scotswood Bridge Junction to more than 800 feet at Consett North Junction in

Rowlands Gill: In this early 20th-century view looking north, a large crowd awaits the arrival of a train to Newcastle. John Mann collection

Rowlands Gill: The exterior of the disused station building in May 1972. *Alan Young*

just over 11 miles. The ruling gradient was 1 in 66, with a short haul of 1 in 63 at the Consett end. The challenges of building in the deep, meandering Derwent valley were exacerbated by having to avoid the grounds of Gibside, home of the Bowes family. This diversion involved the construction of two viaducts across the river, north and south of Rowlands Gill, and the excavation of a cutting half a mile long and 60 feet deep north of the station – but it did mean that Rowlands Gill was served by the line.

North of the station Lockhaugh (or Gibside) Viaduct was 170 yards in length, with nine arches, and built for only a single track, while the double-track Rowlands Gill Viaduct required seven arches and soared 80 feet above the river. Elsewhere on the line there were two further viaducts, deep cuttings and tall embankments. Apart from the double-track section from just north of Rowlands Gill to Lintz Green, the line was single, though later a second track was

Rowlands Gill: Another view from May 1972 shows the style of building found at several stations on the Derwent Valley branch. *Alan Young*

laid northwards to Scotswood Junction, and at High Westwood in connection with the opening of the station in 1909.

When the railway arrived at Rowlands Gill there was little settlement in the locality. The Ordnance Survey map of 1896 shows little but the Towneley Arms public house adjacent to the station, and Cowan Terrace of about 30 cottages, built for miners, with its Primitive Methodist chapel about 500 yards to the north. In 1886 the station booked 31,672 passengers, but the expansion of mining and housing at Rowlands Gill increased its bookings to 130,633 in 1919. In that decade the railway was at its busiest, both for passenger and goods traffic, with regular consignments of coal, iron ore, bricks and timber. In 1910 12 trains left Rowlands Gill for Newcastle on weekdays – six of them operating from Durham, via Lanchester – with two on Sundays. Twelve trains travelled southwards to Blackhill, with an extra on Wednesdays and Saturdays, and two trains on Sundays. By the summer of 1920 there had been a slight reduction in weekday service frequency, but there were three Sunday trains. However, by 1930 the frequency had increased, rising to 15 advertised northbound trains on weekdays, and 17 southbound in the winter of 1937-38; considering that (in 1930) Venture buses offered a service from Rowlands Gill to Newcastle, and to Blackhill and Consett, every 20 minutes on Mondays to Fridays and Sundays, and every 10 minutes on Saturdays, it is remarkable that the frequency of trains had been increased.

Rowlands Gill station's passenger bookings fell to 84,181 in 1921 and only 23,328 in 1930. In the summer of 1948 the service was reduced to only five from Rowlands Gill to Newcastle on Mondays to Fridays, and six in the opposite direction. In 1951 only 724 passengers were booked, and at Ebchester and Shotley Bridge the figures were 98 and 64 respectively; these two stations closed in September 1953, followed by Lintz Green and Swalwell in November. In its final appearance in the timetable Rowlands Gill had one morning train in each direction, and two more from Newcastle calling at 12.38pm and 5.53pm. The line and Rowlands Gill, the last surviving intermediate station between Scotswood and Blackhill, closed to passengers on 1 February

1954, though goods continued to be handled until 11 November 1963, when the line was closed entirely up to Blackhill. Collieries that had contributed traffic to the Derwent valley line had closed by then, and scrap iron from Tyneside ship-breakers' yards to Consett steel mills had been the principal goods traffic. The rails were removed in 1964-65.

Rowlands Gill had two platforms about 110 yards in length. The main building with all the passenger facilities, together with a lamps-and-porters' room, was on the east platform. Built of brick, it was single-storey, and on the platform elevation were twin pavilions, each having a square bay window, with a brick dado and wood above; an extension to the south spoiled the symmetry of the building. A glazed awning stretched between the pavilions. On the front elevation the pavilions extended only a little way forward of the general building line, and the window openings had shallow segmental arches. On the opposite platform an enclosed brick shed was provided, with a long range of windows under a ridged roof. The station master's house was detached and away from the platform, a curious three-storey structure of pale bricks, with a half-hipped roof, arched windows and a bay window to match those on the station building. At the north end of each platform a flight of steps led up to the road bridge by which passengers could cross the line. The signal box was beyond the bridge, allowing the signalman to observe the junction with the Garesfield colliery line, but not the goods sidings and warehouse, which were behind the main building.

The platforms and derelict station building survived into the 1970s, but the west platform shelter had gone. The station master's house has remained in residential use, while only fragments of one platform remain for walkers and cyclists on the old railway track to admire.

BIRTLEY (1868)

Date opened	1 December 1868
Location	Immediately south of Station Lane bridge
Company on opening	North Eastern Railway
Date closed to passengers	5 December 1955
Date closed completely	6 November 1967
Company on closing	Passenger services: British Railways (North Eastern Region) Complete closure: British Rail (Eastern Region)
Present state	Demolished
County	County Durham
OS Grid Ref	NZ267556

The Team Valley line between Newcastle and Durham opened in 1868, followed by the route onward to Ferryhill in 1872. From that time principal trains between Newcastle and York were transferred from the 'old main line' via Leamside and Shincliffe to travel through Durham on the present-day East Coast Main Line. Stations on the new line were at Gateshead West, Low Fell, Lamesley, Birtley, Chester-le-Street and Plawsworth, with Bensham added in 1892.

Birtley originally had two side platforms, with its main building on the up (east) side. This was of a design widely used by the NER, which Biddle describes as a 'dull, but substantial, villa [which] could have been transplanted from any Victorian middle-class suburb from the 1860s onward.' Built of brick, it had an H-plan, with single-storey pavilions at each end, and a

two-storey villa between them. Each pavilion had a canted bay window on the platform, and the villa had a centrally placed cross-gable.

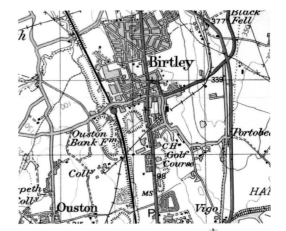

Birtley: Looking north in 1959, shortly after closure of the station, the main building of 1868 is on the right. The enlargement of the station in 1903 to accommodate the Consett-line traffic included construction of the overtrack building. *John Mann collection*

A sloping glass verandah stretched between the pavilions. A waiting shelter stood opposite on the down platform.

On 1 February 1894 the Annfield Plain branch opened, leaving the main line at Ouston Junction, south of Birtley, and providing additional trains that called at Birtley. The extension of this branch to Consett and Blackhill in 1896 and the increased frequency of services on the line led the NER to seek powers to add an extra pair of tracks from Low Fell to Ouston Junction; the work was authorised in 1897. As a result Low Fell, Lamesley and Birtley stations were remodelled, with two side platforms and a central island.

Birtley: The derelict station building, and the Station Hotel beyond it, are seen from a passing train in July 1973. *Alan Young*

In 1903 work was completed at Birtley, including the addition of a timber overtrack building, perched asymmetrically over the new tracks adjacent to the Station Lane bridge. A covered way and staircase led down to the east platform, with covered staircases to the west and island platforms. The island platform received modest timber buildings.

Birtley was a thriving industrial area in the early 20th century. The *Railway Clearing House Handbook* (1904) lists more than 20 industrial establishments in the vicinity that were rail-connected. There was a single-storey, brick-built goods warehouse, and the five lines in the goods yard could accommodate 83 wagons. Bricks and iron and steel were the major goods handled. At that time the station served a population of almost 12,000, and 139,188 tickets were booked in 1911.

The station's site away from the centre of the village began to be a disadvantage after the First World War. Frequent bus services on the Great North Road towards Gateshead, Newcastle and Durham were far more convenient for most residents. Nevertheless the frequency of trains calling at Birtley was maintained. Main-line expresses did not stop, but in 1937-38 11 weekday and four Sunday trains called en route to Durham, and 11 on most weekdays (12 on Wednesdays, 15 on Saturdays), plus two on Sundays, stopped before turning

off towards Consett. This service frequency had changed little since the early 1920s. In 1951 passenger bookings had slumped to only 2,377, and the southbound train service was reduced to six on Monday to Friday, seven on Saturday, and one Sunday working to Durham, with five on weekdays only towards Consett. Birtley's Sunday service was withdrawn during the winter 1951-52 timetable. The service was further reduced on the main line in the winter of 1954-55, and all but one of the Consett-line trains omitted the Birtley stop. The Consett line closed to passengers on 23 May 1955, following which Birtley was left with one northbound and two southbound trains in its final months. Passenger services were withdrawn on 5 December 1955, but goods continued to be handled for almost 12 years, after which Birtley was reduced to the status of a public delivery siding.

The west and island platforms and the overtrack building were demolished soon after closure, but the eastern platform remained in a partially demolished state, with the station building intact and a row of decapitated gas-lamps, until the mid-1960s. The condition of the building deteriorated, and it was demolished some time after 1973. Main-line trains continue to race through the site of Birtley station, but there is little evidence that it ever existed.

LANGLEY (1869)

Ticket: N.E.R. Staward | STAWARD TO LANGLEY | N.E.R. Staward — Langley Fare 1½d. — Langley Fare 1½d. — THIRD CLASS THIRD — Issued subject regulations in time tables — 7941 7941

Date opened	1 March 1869
Location	Immediately east of B6295 about 200 yards from junction with A686
Company on opening	North Eastern Railway
Date closed to passengers	22 September 1930
Date closed completely	20 November 1950
Company on closing	Passenger services: London & North Eastern Railway Goods services: British Railways (North Eastern Region)
Present state	Platform, building and trackbed have been developed as The Garden Station; station house is privately occupied.
County	Northumberland
OS Grid Ref	NY829612

Langley was one of four stations on the 12¼-mile Allendale branch, which climbed from the Tyne valley at Border Counties Junction near Hexham through sparsely populated uplands to Catton in the East Allen Valley. Today this is quiet, pastoral countryside, but 150 years ago lead-mining thrived in the area, and producers and landowners campaigned for rail access. The Hexham & Allendale Railway route was surveyed in 1864 and received the Royal Assent on 19 June 1865. The enabling Act permitted the section from Allendale Town to Allenheads to be omitted if financial or other problems were encountered. The North Eastern Railway was enthusiastic, subscribing £10,000 to the initial cost.

The Engineer, Thomas J. Bewick, faced the task of taking the railway from about 150 feet to almost 800 feet across hilly terrain. Much of the single-track route required cuttings or embankments and tight curves, and trains faced a punishing gradient of up to 1 in 50 for the 7¾ miles from Border Counties

Junction to Langley. A similar climb confronted trains from the southern terminus to Staward. The Allenheads extension would be equally challenging to build.

On 19 August 1867 the line opened to goods, minerals and livestock from Hexham to Langley, and to Catton Road – almost a mile short of Allendale Town – on 13 January 1868. Passenger services provided by the NER commenced on 1 March 1869, serving intermediate stations at Elrington, Langley and Staward. Regrettably, by 1870 the lead industry was declining; jobs in mines and smelters were lost, and the population drifted away. Langley and Allendale smelters had closed by the mid-1880s. The population of Allendale parish fell

Langley: The passenger building and station house are clearly shown in this view, probably from the early 20th century. *John Mann collection*

from 6,401 in 1861 to approximately 2,000 in 1911. In this harsh economic climate it was decided not to extend the branch any further. The Hexham & Allendale was bought out by the NER on 13 July 1876; the NER considered building the short distance to Allendale Town, but abandoned the idea, and Catton Road remained the terminus – renamed Allendale in 1898.

Signalling on the branch was unsophisticated. In the absence of signal boxes, ground frames, operated by the guard or porter, controlled passing loops at each station and permitted access to sidings.

For a little over 60 years a modest service of passenger trains operated. In 1920 there were three workings in each direction on weekdays, with an extra afternoon train on Tuesdays (Hexham's market day) from Hexham to Allendale and back; the service had changed little since the branch was opened. Thirty-three minutes were allowed for the Hexham to Allendale journey, and 3 minutes less for the return. Hexham-based 0-4-4 or 2-4-2 locomotives normally worked the trains. Goods traffic included milk, lead products, livestock, fodder, timber, coal, stone, and general merchandise.

The lonely countryside provided few passengers: Langley booked only 2,976 passengers in 1911. Ticket sales on the branch had changed little by 1923, but by 1929 they declined by more than 70%. In June 1930 the LNER reviewed the viability of the branch and acknowledged that buses had caused financial problems. Robert Emmerson ran buses at 2-hourly intervals between Newcastle, Hexham and Allendale Town, while Wharton's buses plied at 75-minute intervals between Hexham, Haydon Bridge, Langley, Catton and Allendale Town. The fastest buses equalled the train journey time, but linked the centres of Hexham and Allendale, rather than their inconveniently sited stations. Emmerson was a subsidiary of United, an associated company of the LNER, and the review assumed that a considerable

proportion of the rail loss would accrue to that company. Herein is a reminder that railway companies sometimes had a financial interest in what appeared to be their competitors. The review concluded that because of the marked decline in traffic 'it seems clear that any complaints from the public regarding the withdrawal of the passenger train service can be readily dealt with'.

On 22 September 1930 passenger services ended, but goods traffic continued. From 29 July 1936 Langley station was renamed Langley-on-Tyne. The line closed completely on 20 November 1950, and the rails were lifted. Much of the branch can be traced today, and from Glendue Siding to Langley the trackbed is a footpath.

The two-platform Langley station served a small community, Langley Castle, and a rail-connected lead smelter. The station house beside the up platform presents a brick gable-end to the platform, and has a rather ungainly, rendered pent-roofed addition extending to three storeys where the ground falls away from the platforms. Passenger facilities on the up platform were in a wooden shed with a pitched roof, central sliding door, and flanking windows; the down platform handled goods and parcels. After serving for many years as a post office, the former passenger shed has a new use. Together with the platforms and trackbed, it has been transformed by Jane Torday into The Garden Station. Gardening courses are held there, and plants are for sale. Her aim was 'to preserve the sense of a secret garden hidden in the woods'.

Langley: At what is now known as The Garden Station, horticultural courses are held and plants are sold. The trackbed for a short distance towards Hexham is included as part of a woodland garden. This view is from March 2002. *Alan Young*

NORTH WYLAM (1876)

Date opened	13 May 1876
Location	Between Falcon Terrace and Main Road, just north of road bridge over River Tyne, less than 5 minutes' walk from Wylam station
Company on opening	Scotswood, Newburn & Wylam Railway & Dock Company (worked from the outset by the North Eastern Railway)
Date closed to passengers	11 March 1968
Date closed completely	11 March 1968
Company on closing	British Rail (Eastern Region)
Present state	Parts of a platform is in situ
County	Northumberland
OS Grid Ref	NZ118647

A curious feature of the Newcastle to Carlisle line was a choice of routes between Scotswood and Prudhoe. From September 1958 the northern route had only one station on it – North Wylam – less than 5 minutes' walk from Wylam station on the southern route, the other three stations having closed. The reasons for the development of these parallel routes have been outlined in the chapter on Scotswood station (1848).

Despite being a loop line from Scotswood to Prudhoe, passenger trains from Newcastle generally terminated at North Wylam, a practice that continued until the 1950s. In 1889 a complaint by a passenger, whose journey from Heddon-on-the-Wall involved a transfer with luggage between Wylam's stations to reach Prudhoe or stations west, failed to impress NER officials.

The 1898 timetable showed six passenger trains each way between Newcastle and North Wylam (terminus) at irregular intervals, with a few additional services on certain days. Goods train workings were also apparently confined to the section east of North Wylam, although an express meat train from Carlisle was routed along the loop. Otherwise Wylam Bridge presumably carried only mineral trains, relieving congestion on the Wylam-Blaydon line.

North Wylam: The station staff pose on the south platform circa 1900. A delightful array of plants adorns the north platform, from which trains departed for Newcastle. *John Mann collection*

In 1920 ten trains operated each way on weekdays between Newcastle and North Wylam. By the winter of 1937-38 the service had strengthened to approximately half-hourly trains on weekdays and hourly on Sundays. In 1955 British Railways promoted the loop to 'through' status, with several passenger trains each day over Wylam Bridge. From 1955 to 1968 passenger trains on the route were at irregular intervals. In June 1965 on Monday to Friday six westbound trains called at North Wylam, with five on Saturdays. In the opposite direction there were nine on Monday to Friday and six on Saturdays. From that month Sunday trains used the loop, with nine westbound and 12 eastbound trains calling at North Wylam rather than at Blaydon and Wylam.

In 1958 British Railways took the apparently illogical step of closing Lemington, Newburn and Heddon-on-the-Wall stations (all of which had no alternative station to use), yet retaining North Wylam. However, 1951 traffic statistics show that North Wylam was the busiest of the four stations on the loop: 37,197 tickets were issued there, but fewer than 25,000 for the other three stations combined. At that time, moreover, North Wylam was effectively a terminus without traffic to or from the west, and its bookings exceeded those at Wylam (30,261). North Wylam closed to goods traffic

on 2 January 1961, then in 1963 Beeching recommended the closure of 13 Newcastle-Carlisle passenger stations, including Scotswood and North Wylam. According to Map 9 in the Report, passenger services would continue to use the North Wylam loop – with no station remaining at which to stop – while 'stopping' services would cease to use the route via Blaydon, and Wylam and Blaydon stations would close too.

In 1966 BR decided that North Wylam station should remain open, but that the route via Blaydon should close. This was justified by the expense of maintaining Scotswood Bridge, 'certain advantages' of the North Wylam route for freight working, declining business at Blaydon, and the ease of transferring Wylam's passenger business 300 yards to North Wylam.

Trains between Scotswood and Prudhoe via Wylam were suspended from 3 September 1966 for engineering work associated with the building of a new road crossing of the River Tyne at Scotswood. As a result, until May 1967, when services via Blaydon were restored, all trains travelled via North Wylam. In 1967 North Wylam booked 34,698 passengers, a figure inflated by the temporary closure of Wylam station.

BR's proposal in 1966 to close Wylam but retain North Wylam was rejected, so proceedings began in 1967 to close the North Wylam loop. North Wylam station was profitable, with annual passenger receipts of £4,650 against operating costs of £2,100, but abandonment from North Stella (Newburn) to West Wylam Junction, including the bridge over the River Tyne, would save an estimated £8,500 in maintenance and renewal. Whereas BR had emphasised the operating advantages

North Wylam: The station is seen in 1951, looking west, showing the signal box and range of passenger buildings. At this time trains still terminated here, rather than continuing over West Wylam Bridge towards Hexham. *Alan Young collection*

North Wylam: A fully flanged totem sign from the station. *Richard Furness images*

North Wylam: On Saturday 9 March 1968 – the last weekend of services – a Carlisle to Newcastle train calls at 17.44. *Alan Young*

of the North Wylam loop a year earlier, now – remarkably – its disadvantages emerged! North Wylam had speed restrictions owing to 'sharp curves, gradients, and poor foundations' (the maximum gradient was a very short stretch at 1 in 85) and would be expensive to upgrade to trunk route standards. Of course, the passenger traffic that could have readily switched from Wylam to North Wylam could now be justified in reverse. Valiant protesters opposed the closure, including Northumberland County Council. Grounds for objection included the proximity of North Wylam station to a planned housing estate, the unpleasant walk over the bridge to Wylam station in inclement weather, and the inconvenient layout and poor condition of that station. However, closure was inevitable. The TUCC Report of 12 September 1967 concluded that Wylam (population 1,495) did not warrant two stations, and that passengers used either station 'according to which particular train suits their immediate requirements'.

On 11 March 1968 passenger traffic ceased on the loop and North Wylam closed. On Saturday 9 March (the penultimate day of service) there was a sense of 'business as

normal' – no signs of impending doom, or special events as were seen on some other lines immediately prior to closure. Rails through North Wylam were retained until April 1972, when the line was cut back to Newburn. The Scotswood-Newburn section was taken out of use in December 1986. Most of the loop is a cycle route and footpath (Tyne Riverside Country Park). Stephenson's Cottage, the birthplace of George Stephenson in 1781, stands alongside the former railway a short distance east of North Wylam, and is an enduring feature of interest.

North Wylam station possessed two 130-yard platforms. The brick buildings were uninspired single-storey structures. The main one on the down platform contained (from west to east) a porters' room, booking and parcels office, general and ladies' waiting rooms, and a lamp-room with gentlemen's toilet behind. A signal box was on the platform, east of the building. The up platform had a pent-roof enclosed waiting shed and toilet. Goods facilities were south of the main building. A concrete footbridge was added to the ensemble in about 1960. Until closure the station was gas-lit, and it was the only one on the loop line that definitely had BR totem signs installed. When the rails through North Wylam were removed in 1972 the station was still substantially intact, but much of it has subsequently been demolished.

North Wylam: In January 1973 the platforms, passenger buildings and concrete footbridge (circa 1960) remained in place, but the rails and signal box had disappeared. *Alan Young*

North Wylam: The station site looking south-west in June 2009. *Ali Ford*

DEADWATER (1880)

L. N. E. R.

FOR CONDITIONS SEE BACK. Available for three days, including day of issue.

DEADWATER   to

SAUGHTREE

Fare   S   6½d C
THIRD / 151 \ CLASS
       SAUGHTREE

Date opened	Private use by 1877; open to the public 1 March 1880
Location	At end of 100-yard track west of unclassified Kielder to Saughtree road
Company on opening	North British Railway
Date closed to passengers	15 October 1956
Date closed completely	15 October 1956
Company on closing	British Railways (North Eastern Region)
Present state	Platform intact and station building divided into two residences
County	Northumberland
OS Grid Ref	NY603968

In *The Romance of Northumberland* (1908) A. G. Bradley wrote 'In a wild hollow under the English slope [of Peel Fell] the North Tyne springs from peat mosses, and on its way down lingers silently for a time in a rushy flat known to the borderers as Deadwater, a name now embalmed in the timetables of the North British Railway.'

He refers to the 'Lilliputian station with a narrow platform' whose outlook is 'wild, solitary and beautiful, incidentally disclosing a couple of farmhouses and perhaps twice as many cottages.' He notes, with surprise, that when he alighted there a young woman was in charge of the station.

Deadwater: On 13 October 1956 (the final day of passenger services) No 77011 leaves Scotland and enters England with a Hawick to Newcastle train. *Alan Brown collection*

A few yards from Scotland, a timber platform – Deadwater Foot Crossing – was built on the north-east side of the tracks and close to a siding, to serve quarry workers. In 1880, as Deadwater, it became a public station, with a lengthened platform and an austere single-storey stone building. The isolated spot provided few passengers: Bradley pondered 'who uses it, I cannot imagine'. Yet the station survived until the line closed in 1956, albeit unstaffed from 19

Above left **Deadwater:** Looking south-east on the same day. *Alan Brown collection*

Left **Deadwater:** In May 1972 the platform and building remain in remarkably good condition. *Alan Young*

Above right **Deadwater:** In April 2009 the platform in the foreground has been reconstructed – compare with the similar view in 1956. The building, in residential use, has undergone some alteration, but the character of this remote station has been retained. A. G. Bradley, who visited the station 100 years earlier, would recognise it. *Alan Young*

September 1955, the date when it ceased to handle goods traffic.

In its later years Deadwater's timetable had some charming eccentricities. From 1948 to 1952 on alternate Saturdays, late-night trains ran (1952 timings) from Hexham (departing 10.30pm) to Kielder Forest (arriving 11.54pm) and from Hawick (departing 10.57pm) to Falstone (arriving 12.07 on Sunday morning). This allowed remote communities at Falstone, Plashetts, Lewiefield Halt and Kielder to visit the cinema alternately in the closest English and Scottish towns. Deadwater's residents were therefore permitted a fortnightly Scottish Saturday night in Hawick, but not an English one in Hexham. How many revellers alighted at a quarter to midnight at the oil-lit platform amid empty moorlands? After 1952 the Hawick-Falstone train was withdrawn, denying these isolated folk one of life's pleasures. From about 1946 passengers wishing to join the 6.55am southbound train had to contact the station master at Riccarton Junction before 5.00pm the previous day. One wonders how many requests he received, and why this procedure was followed, rather than simply timetabling the train to stop.

When the line closed in 1956, buses already plied between Hexham and Bellingham, but no operator was willing to serve the scattered communities between Bellingham and Riccarton. The British Transport Commission persuaded Norman Fox Motors to provide a replacement service with a subsidy for three years. So the firm's elderly United vehicles began to run between Bellingham and Kielder, extended to Deadwater and Steele Road (on the 'Waverley route') on Saturdays. Sadly, the Transport Users' Consultative Committee file of correspondence regarding local dissatisfaction with the replacement buses is a weighty one.

Deadwater station is in an excellent state of preservation, well worth visiting to relive Bradley's experience of a century ago – minus the trains.

WHITTINGHAM (1887)

Date opened	5 September 1887
Location	On north side of minor road immediately east of its junction with A697
Company on opening	North Eastern Railway
Date closed to passengers	22 September 1930
Date closed completely	2 March 1953
Company on closing	Passenger services: London & North Eastern Railway Goods services: British Railways (North Eastern Region)
Present state	In agricultural use, and in a remarkable state of preservation. Signal box and water tower have been demolished; building on island platform derelict; goods shed in agricultural use; degraded goods platform survives, as do coal cells and weigh house. Station cottages east of line in private occupation.
County	Northumberland
OS Grid Ref	NU089121

Whittingham and the other intermediate stations on the Alnwick & Cornhill Railway were built on a lavish scale, and every one survives, 80 years after the line closed to passengers. This remarkable survival rate reflects the quality of their buildings, which is unsurpassed by any other minor rural line in Britain. The station masters enjoyed some of the finest residences in this part of Northumberland, perhaps as recompense for

being posted to such a remote area. Addyman and Mallon (2007) suggest that the extravagant buildings were designed to placate major landowners, or to show the rival North British Railway how to build decent Northumbrian stations; the NBR's intermediate stations on the Rothbury branch were somewhat spartan. However, the optimism and profitability of the NER in the 1880s must not be overlooked, and it is worth noting that in the following decades new NER station buildings in rural areas were far less opulent.

The first passenger railway to enter northern Northumberland was the East Coast Main Line. Having opened from Newcastle to Tweedmouth in 1847, it reached Berwick in 1850. The line avoided the Duke of Northumberland's estate at Alnwick, but a branch line from Alnmouth reached the town, opening in 1850. From Tweedmouth a railway opened between 1849 and 1851 up Tweeddale to Cornhill (whose station was renamed

Whittingham: The island platform with its building, and the goods warehouse, looking north in January 1976. *Alan Young*

Coldstream in 1873), Kelso and St Boswells. The countryside between this line and Alnwick, where the lonely Cheviot Hills sweep down to the fertile valleys of the Breamish, Till and Bowmont, was not to welcome a railway until 1887.

Whittingham, Wooler and other villages in these valleys could have been served by rail much earlier had the NBR Northumberland Central Railway scheme of 1862 been completed. This line was to approach Wooler from the south, but never progressed north of Rothbury, owing in part to objections from Alnwick

Whittingham: The elaborate brackets supporting the awning and the uncoursed sandstone construction of the building can be appreciated in this view from August 2001. *Alan Young*

businessmen, who feared losing trade to Wooler. In 1881 the Central Northumberland Railway was proposed from Newcastle to Wooler, following a similar route north of Rothbury to the 1862 scheme; again, Alnwick's commercial interests would not be served. However (also in 1881), the NER expressed its intention to

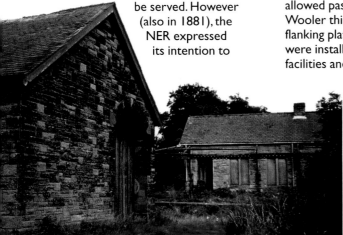

construct the Alnwick & Cornhill Railway, which received the Royal Assent in 1882.

This 35-mile route opened from Alnwick to Wooperton for goods on 2 May 1887, and on 5 September passenger services began on the entire line. Rather than head north for Wooler via the gentle gradients of the Aln valley, from Alnwick the line pursued a difficult course over Alnwick Moor, with tight curves, almost continuous 1 in 50 gradients, a 351-yard tunnel, and a five-arch viaduct on a horseshoe bend at Edlingham – all, it would appear, to include Whittingham in its progress to Wooler. In fact, the railway missed Whittingham by more than a mile, but a station was provided at its closest approach to the village. The principal reason for the diversion towards Whittingham was that the railway did not have to encroach on the ducal estate surrounding Alnwick Castle. North of Whittingham the route was almost direct to Wooler, accompanying the Morpeth to Coldstream road (A697).

The Alnwick & Cornhill stations were designed by William Bell, the NER's architect from 1877 to 1914. In the opinion of the authority on NER architecture, Bill Fawcett (2005), 'Impeccably crafted in local stone by the line's contractors, Meakin & Dean, the stations, cottages, goods sheds and specially designed signal boxes seem to provide an exemplar of what … a well-designed country branch line should be.' Whittingham station was unusual in having the only island platform on the A&C route, and being the only one with this layout on any of the NER's single-track lines. The platform arrangement allowed passenger trains to cross, though at Wooler this was achieved with conventional flanking platforms, and goods passing loops were installed at all other stations. Passenger facilities and offices on Whittingham's platform were in a long, rather plain single-storey building with a slate ridged roof and rectangular mullioned windows, but distinction was added by the shallow, glazed awning that surrounded it. The brackets

Whittingham: The goods and passenger buildings in August 2001. *Alan Young*

carrying the awning were adorned with the Star of David – a motif used in the ironwork of some other contemporary NER stations. Inside the booking hall the NER, in its optimism, provided two booking windows, with 'in' and 'out' notices on either side, to ensure that the anticipated crowds formed orderly queues. While at other stations on the line (including Mindrum) the station master's house was on the platform, at Whittingham it stood apart, accompanied by a row of railway cottages. This arrangement proved more expensive; only Wooler, whose combined station house and offices were the largest between Alnwick and Coldstream, cost more to build. A water tank and signal box stood north of the passenger building, east of the track. The large, four-wagon warehouse was on the opposite side of the line, as were the facilities for handling livestock and coal. All of the buildings at Whittingham were of rock-faced sandstone, possibly obtained from the cuttings between Edlingham and Alnwick. After Wooler, this was the busiest station on the line, booking 6,942 passengers in 1911. A variety of traffic was handled, including livestock – a mart adjoined the station – grain, coal, and tiles from Slaters brickworks' siding, to the east of the passenger facilities.

With fewer than 8,000 people to serve along its route, passenger traffic was limited. In 1893 the intermediate stations issued 62,500 tickets, after which business slackened; in 1911 48,870 tickets were issued, declining further to 43,500 in 1922. For much of the line's life there were three trains each way on weekdays (four on Saturdays) stopping at all stations; no trains ran on Sundays. Around 1910 a push-and-pull steam 'autocar' (a 'BTP' tank engine and two or three coaches) operated. In LNER days 'G5', 'D17' and 'D20' Class locomotives were used, based at Tweedmouth shed. Most

of the villages nominally served by the railway, including Whittingham, were some distance from their stations, and several of these stations were beside the A697, therefore particularly vulnerable to bus competition. United (an LNER-associated company) provided direct buses between Newcastle and Wooler – far more convenient than changing trains at Alnwick and Alnmouth – while Allan & Henderson and Western had eight weekday, ten Saturday and three Sunday services between Alnwick and Wooler. Western buses stopped in Whittingham village, sparing its inhabitants the half-hour walk to the station. The railway closed to passengers on 22 September 1930 and settled down to a quiet life as a goods line.

Passenger trains continued to visit the branch occasionally. From 1935 a camping coach was available at Whittingham for holidaymakers, who were expected to reach it by rail; this was achieved by attaching a passenger coach to Saturday parcels trains. At the outbreak of the Second World War the remote Northumbrian countryside was considered safe for young evacuees, for whom special passenger services were provided, and RAF Millfield, near Akeld, also required troop trains to run. After the war, on 12 August 1948, a severe storm caused flooding in the Borders, temporarily closing the East Coast Main Line north of Berwick, while the A&C line was damaged in several places, notably between Mindrum and Kirknewton, where a bridge over Kilham Burn was destroyed. Other damage was repaired, and goods services resumed north from Mindrum, and south through Wooler and Whittingham to Alnwick. In October 1949 floods severed the line where it crossed Lilburn Burn between Ilderton and Wooler, and BR decided not to reopen this section, but to restore the bridge near Kirknewton; thereafter Whittingham was on a branch, from Alnwick to Ilderton, but only until 2 March 1953, when the line was abandoned. The Wooler to Coldstream goods line survived until 29 March 1965.

Whittingham has one of the finest collections of buildings to be found at a lost station and is well worth a visit.

Whittingham: The weigh office and coal cells, west of the passenger station, in August 2001. *Alan Young*

MINDRUM (1887)

Mindrum: In this view from 1950 the station remains in use for goods traffic. The lavish stone villa with its glazed wooden verandah, and the goods warehouse, were typical features of stations on this rural byway. *John Mann collection*

Date opened	5 September 1887
Location	North side of unnamed minor road immediately east of its junction with A697
Company on opening	North Eastern Railway
Date closed to passengers	22 September 1930
Date closed completely	29 March 1965
Company on closing	Passenger services: London & North Eastern Railway Goods services: British Rail (North Eastern Region)
Present state	Main station building is in residential use; goods shed survives within a scrapyard; some railway cottages also in private occupation.
County	Northumberland
OS Grid Ref	NT854339

With its fine, well-preserved stations, the Alnwick & Cornhill line deserves a second entry. Mindrum, the most northerly intermediate station, represents the style of building found at five of the stations, the others being Glanton, Hedgeley, Wooperton and Ilderton.

Mindrum station was located where the line emerged from a deep valley at the foot of the Cheviot Hills and entered the broad, fertile valley of the Tweed. It served three hamlets –

Mindrum, Mindrummill and Pawston – within 2 miles, the Scottish villages of Town Yetholm and Kirk Yetholm, 4 miles to the south, and a number of isolated farms. The principal goods traffic was agricultural, notably barley and livestock; coal and coke were also handled, as at most British stations. The amount of goods traffic handled, in terms of tonnage, was among the highest for stations on the Alnwick & Cornhill line from its opening until 1914.

The main building at its single passenger

Left **Mindrum:** The exterior of the station in January 1976. *Alan Young*

Below **Mindrum:** The platform elevation, seen in August 2001. *Alan Young*

Below left **Mindrum:** An exterior view including the goods platform and warehouse, also in August 2001. *Alan Young*

platform consisted of a stone two-storey villa, largely given over to the station master's accommodation, with an attached single-storey office range. The slate roofs were half-hipped, as were the two gabled windows facing the platform, and three on the exterior elevation. Tall chimneystacks and iron finials gave a final touch of elegance to the roof. A large, single gable (not half- hipped) on the exterior of the offices stood forward and overlapped the two-storey villa, providing visual unity between the two elements of the building. Passengers were sheltered by a herringbone-patterned glazed, wooden verandah that extended the length of the platform frontage, with partitions at each end for a general waiting room and a gentlemen's waiting room. (The ladies' waiting room was within the structure of the villa.) The verandah possibly detracted from the dignity of the stone buildings, but added to their distinctiveness and to passenger comfort. At the back of the platform south of the building a sandstone wall with curved coping stones was provided.

Mindrum station's layout permitted one passenger and one goods train, or two goods trains, to pass. Its signal cabin was closed in 1901 and replaced with a 'dwarf frame' housed in an extension to the station verandah; the telegraph instruments were moved to the booking office.

Today the station building has received a single-storey extension at its northern end, and conservatories on the exterior and platform elevations. (At Akeld there is a full platform verandah in NER style.) Only one of the chimneystacks remains, reduced in height, but most of the gables still have finials. The passenger platform has been removed, but both the goods platform and goods shed survive.

CARVILLE (1891)

Date opened	1 August 1891
Location	South of Hadrian Road, close to junction with Park Road, about 300 yards east of Wallsend Metro station
Company on opening	North Eastern Railway
Date closed to passengers	23 July 1973
Date closed completely	23 July 1973 (goods facilities, known as Wallsend, closed 11 July 1966)
Company on closing	British Rail (Eastern Region)
Present state	Demolished, but signal box base and railway cottages survive
County	Northumberland (now Tyne & Wear)
OS Grid Ref	NZ303662

The 6½-mile Riverside branch (actually a loop) was authorised on 13 July 1871 from Riverside Junction, between Manors East and Heaton, to Percy Main. The line served industries and communities on the north bank of the Tyne that the direct Manors-North Shields line missed. It opened on 1 May 1879 with stations at St Peters, St Anthonys, Low Walker (Walker from 13 May 1889) and Willington Quay. Carville, Byker and Point Pleasant were later additions. The scenery was unashamedly urban and industrial, but it was a fascinating journey, with two tunnels, high embankments, a deep cutting, and a viaduct over Willington Dene. Massive cranes, and vessels under construction or repair, could be admired in the shipyards that adjoined the route, and there were glimpses of the River Tyne. In its closing years the series of semi-derelict, officially 'staffed' stations added to the character of the journey. It is unfortunate that few railway photographers visited the line, or travelled on its last trains.

Within two years of the electrification of the local tramways in 1901 there was a 40%

Carville: On Friday 20 June 1969 numerous passengers await the arrival of one of the two late-afternoon trains towards the coast. *John Mann*

Left **Carville:** A diesel multiple unit on a Newcastle-Coast circular calls on Tuesday 6 June 1972 at 16.43 en route to the coast to collect shipyard workers. This was the only advertised eastbound train in the evening, but an unadvertised workmen's train to West Monkseaton would call at 18.42. *Alan Young*

Below **Carville:** The station building, signal box and station cottages are seen in December 1972. The short wooden glazed verandah formerly extended the full length of the recessed area between the wings of the building. *Alan Young*

reduction in passenger bookings on the north Tyneside suburban railways. The North Eastern Railway swiftly responded by electrifying these lines on a third-rail 600V DC system, beginning with a trial run between Carville and Percy Main on 27 September 1903; on 1 July 1904 electrification from Newcastle to the coast, including the Riverside, was complete. Steam traction was retained for goods movement. Electric trains ran until 1967, when diesel multiple units took over the service.

The main building at the four original stations – St Peters, St Anthonys, Walker and Willington Quay – was a single-storey, H-plan brick structure. Carville station was a little more ambitious, though plans to include an arched portico and a small tower were abandoned. The single-storey main building was at the west end of the down platform. The frontage was straight and had a large, decorated central gable with a finial over the entrance. The pitched roofline of the cross-wings on the platform side ended in half-hipped gables on the frontage. At the east end of the building, looking like an afterthought, was a further section that reversed the roof details of the pavilions, with a half-hipped end facing the platform and a gable end on the frontage. Because the platforms were on a tight curve and the building was straight and parallel to the road it fronted, the

Carville: The grimy exterior of the station is seen on Sunday 8 July 1973, a fortnight before closure. The entrance to the building is locked; it was open for a short time on Monday to Friday mornings and late afternoons when tickets were issued for the few trains that called. Although the market for redundant enamel station signage was already active, and tangerine North Eastern Region specimens were particularly in demand, even by the late 1970s no one had relieved Carville of the nameboard over the entrance or the British Railways sign on the poster boards – the photographer resisted temptation! *Alan Young*

west end of the platform was progressively wider towards the ramp. Conversely, at the eastern end of the main building, the additional section under a half-hipped roof was recessed, so as not to make the platform dangerously narrow. On the platform, serving as a waiting room, a glazed verandah with a lean-to roof stretched between the cross-wings, and above its central entrance on the platform side was a small gable. The two cross-wing gables were decorated with simple wooden finials and pendants, which survived until closure. Inside, white glazed bricks clad the booking hall, and even in its final days the booking office window was opened in the morning and evening rush hours to issue tickets. Beyond the level crossing was a tall brick-built NER signal box with a pitched roof, accompanied by a row of railway cottages. The up platform had a wooden waiting shelter towards its west end.

Signage at Carville in the BR era consisted of a hand-painted wooden nameboard on each platform and LNER nameplates; vitreous enamel nameboards and later 'corporate identity' nameplates were not installed. From 1970 every Riverside station received tall vandal-proof electric lamps to replace the LNER swans-neck lamps. Good lighting was essential, since in mid-winter no trains called in daylight hours.

Despite its proximity to Wallsend station, Carville was not starved of passengers. In the closing years of the branch, Carville was the busiest Riverside station, conveniently situated at the entrance to Wallsend Shipyard. When a siren announced the end of the afternoon shift, hundreds of men poured out of the premises, many onto the platforms at Carville; the station, silent during the day, was crowded for a few minutes.

The main building survived until closure, though only the western end of the glazed verandah was intact. If they had the inclination, passengers could admire a display of pelargoniums on the south-facing waiting room window ledge. There were no buildings on the up platform at closure. In 1979 the station was still largely intact; even the 'British Railways Carville' enamel sign remained on the exterior wall.

In the summer of 1896 trains operated in both directions on weekdays at approximately 2-hourly intervals, increasing by 1910 to hourly every day. Bradshaw of July 1938 shows an hourly service supplemented by extra trains on weekday mornings, in the late-afternoon rush hour on Mondays to Fridays, and at lunchtime on Saturdays – when shipyards closed for the weekend. One train ran each way on Sunday morning. By July 1943 several daytime services had been withdrawn, as had Sunday trains. In BR days the service frequently changed, but it was largely confined to rush hours. The winter of 1953-54 had the scantiest advertised service, with one weekday train to Newcastle direct, and three in the opposite direction. In 1961 the timetable reached its greatest complexity, with variations between weekdays dictated by the shifts of the shipyard workers, who were the main users of the line. A series of simplifications followed, and in October 1971 the service achieved its final austerity of Monday to Friday 07.15 and 16.43 departures for Tynemouth, and 07.18, 08.38 and 16.45 to Newcastle direct. An unadvertised Riverside train left for Tynemouth at 18.42 on Tuesdays, Wednesdays and Thursdays to collect shipyard overtime workers.

Closure of the branch was recommended in the Beeching Report, but it was reprieved in 1964 pending construction of a direct road between Wallsend and Willington Quay. In mid-1972 the road was completed, and closure of the line was again recommended. On 17 April 1973 consent was given on the understanding that replacement bus licences would be obtained by 23 July of that year. There was no special final train for railway enthusiasts. Instead they had to decide which train was the final one! The 16.24 from Newcastle (direct) was the last over the entire branch, while the 16.40 starting from Willington Quay was the last train on Riverside metals. Few people came to pay their last respects.

Goods trains continued, but from 31 May 1978 Carville's Swan Hunter Siding became the eastern terminus, and by July 1979 the rails had been lifted from there to Percy Main. In April 1987 the line was further truncated to St Peters. The last goods train ran on this section on 25 September 1987, and it was taken out of use on 31 March 1988.

Since complete closure all of the stations have been demolished, and some of the trackbed has been erased. Between St Peters and Carville the trackbed is a footpath and cycling route.

Carville: Six years after closure, in July 1979, a track is still in place, but the station is in an advanced state of decay. *Alan Young*

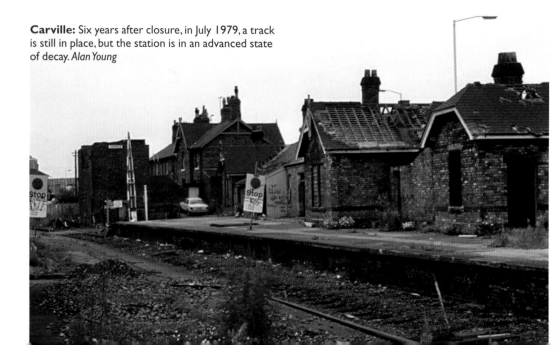

CONSETT (1896)

Date opened	17 August 1896
Location	East side of Delves Lane
Company on opening	North Eastern Railway
Date closed to passengers	23 May 1955
Date closed completely	2 October 1967
Company on closing	Passenger services: British Railways (North Eastern Region) Goods services: British Rail (Eastern Region)
Present state	Demolished; site is lost under new road (A692)
County	County Durham
OS Grid Ref	NZ112507

In the early 19th century, the area of north-western County Durham where the town of Consett would develop was sparsely inhabited windswept moorland, of little agricultural value. However, quantities of iron ore lay beneath the surface, and a Sunderland mineralogist, William Richardson, recognised the economic potential of these resources. In the 1830s-'40s the demand for iron goods was rising, led by the expanding railway system in Britain with its insatiable demand for iron rails. With such a market in mind, Richardson founded the Derwent Iron Company in 1841, close to the recently opened Stanhope & Tyne mineral

Consett: The SLS/RCTS five-day 'North East Railtour' visits the station on 28 September 1963. *Brian Johnson*

Consett: In December 1973 the platform shows signs of deterioration. The sidings still accommodate a large number of coal wagons. *Alan Young*

railway, which ran from upper Weardale to South Shields. The terraced cottages he provided for his workers formed a community originally known as Berry Edge, which developed into the town of Consett. The early years of this iron industry were less than successful, owing in part to the imprudence of a bank with which the company was involved, and it was not until the Derwent Iron Company was taken over (and renamed the Consett Iron Company) that the industry really thrived and the village expanded; the 1891 census recorded 8,760 inhabitants, and by 1951 Consett was a substantial town with a population of almost 39,000. The iron and steel industry grew to dominate the town, economically and visually. Perched on the summit of a steep westward-facing scarp almost 1,000 feet above sea level, the works were visible from many miles away. Vast quantities of furnace slag were dumped on the slope to the west, while the chimneys belched out huge volumes of red dust. The local iron ore proved less abundant than had been expected, and eventually imported ore had to be hauled uphill to Consett from near the mouth of the Tyne. Coal, suitable for coke production, was available in the Pontop coalfield, a few miles north-east of Consett. This was of enormous benefit to the growing iron and steel industry, as was the limestone from upper Weardale.

Consett station, opened in 1896, was not the first to serve the growing community. In 1834 the Stanhope & Tyne 'railroad' had opened to carry limestone and coal. Most of this line was unsuitable for passenger traffic, having numerous extremely steep inclines. However, from the outset local people made informal journeys in the coal wagons, and in 1835 official public trains began to operate between South Shields and Chester-le-Street (Durham Turnpike). When a particularly steep section at Hownes Gill (some 2 miles south-west of Consett) was replaced

with a 150-foot-high viaduct, and a deviation line to avoid Nanny Mayor's incline near Waskerley was built, passenger services began to operate from Crook and Tow Law, past the site of the 1896 Consett station, to terminate at Carr House, where a station opened in 1858.

Consett still did not have a conveniently situated station, or even one bearing its name. However, on 1 September 1862 a passenger and goods line from Durham, via Lanchester and Witton Gilbert, opened to a point about a mile west of Carr House, where the first Consett station was built. It was immediately south of the present A692 road to Castleside, at the southern end of the ironworks site, and, like Carr House, some distance from the main built-up area of Consett. This terminus was short-lived, as the line was extended northwards up the Derwent valley, via Lintz Green, to Newcastle. Consett station closed, to be replaced with Benfieldside, a short distance north, on 2 December 1867. This station was renamed Consett on 1 November 1882, despite being located much closer to Blackhill, a large village that also housed Consett Iron Company workers. On 1 May 1885 it was renamed once more, this time as Consett & Blackhill, before becoming Blackhill on 1 May 1896.

Returning to the route through the final Consett station, the service to Carr House ended on 1 October 1868. During the 1870s and '80s Consett grew rapidly, as did several villages to its east – Leadgate, Annfield Plain and Stanley – which were served by mineral railways, but the absence of a passenger service was resented by their residents. The old Stanhope & Tyne line was still unsuitable for passenger traffic, with two 1 in 27 inclines at Annfield Plain where wagons were rope-hauled by a stationary engine. Eventually, on 23 May 1887, Royal Assent was given for the North Eastern Railway to construct a route avoiding these inclines by means of a broad curve, but even this new line would be steeply graded, much of it at 1 in 51 and 1 in 55, with a short stretch reaching 1 in 35. The double-track diversion and upgraded old route as far as the East Coast Main Line, which it joined at the north-facing Ouston Junction near Birtley, opened to passengers as far as Annfield Plain on 1 February 1894. The existing single mineral line westward was doubled, with some slight realignment and construction of new bridges, and a new curve was built in 1893 from Consett East to North junctions. Passenger services between Annfield Plain and Blackhill began on 17 August 1896, without any formal ceremony, calling at the intermediate stations of Leadgate and Consett.

The 6.10 am from Newcastle to Blackhill was the first train on the opening day. At first there were five trains each way on weekdays, with some additional services east of Annfield Plain. In June 1920 the timetable shows eight trains from Newcastle to Consett on Monday to Friday, six continuing to Blackhill; ten on Saturdays, six continuing to Blackhill; and a further late train on Wednesdays only, terminating at Consett. There were two trains on Sunday in each direction, working to or from Blackhill. Seven trains left Consett for Newcastle on Mondays to Fridays, five originating at Blackhill, and nine on Saturdays, six of which started from Blackhill.

By the 1890s the NER had entered a phase of constructing economical timber buildings at its new stations, but in the case of those between Birtley and Blackhill the risk of damage by mining subsidence also justified the use of lighter structures. At Consett there was one broad island platform on which a long, single-storey timber building with a slate ridged roof accommodated the passenger facilities and offices. There were two small gables midway along the north-west side of the roof. The building was surrounded by a generous flat roofed awning with a deep crenulated valance, in its later years supported at intervals by second-hand rails. A ramp led down to the platform from the road overbridge. A large area of sidings

Consett: The timber building, looking north-east in December 1973. *Alan Young*

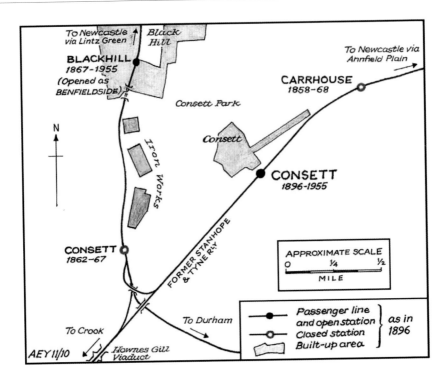

Consett: A map of the railways and stations that served Consett. *Alan Young*

spread to the north-west of the station. Wood was used not only for the station buildings but also for the goods shed and stable. The station master was denied the dignity of a detached dwelling, as at many stations, but had to be content with accommodation at the end of Sherburn Terrace.

It would appear to have been the most important station on the Birtley-Blackhill route, but Consett booked considerably fewer passengers than some of its neighbours. In 1913 the station issued 79,041 tickets, while Annfield Plain and Shield Row (later West Stanley) issued 114,212 and 170,308 respectively. Blackhill station was well situated to serve the steelworks and the north-western area of Consett's urban sprawl, as well as being a four-way junction; for these reasons it greatly exceeded Consett's bookings, issuing 145,849 tickets in 1913.

The town continued to grow in the 20th century, but the use of its station declined after the First World War, principally owing to competition from buses. In 1931 Venture buses operated between Consett and Newcastle (via Rowlands Gill) every 20 minutes, including

Sundays, while Northern bus 33 provided a half-hourly service via Leadgate and Burnopfield. Further Northern buses (service 11 via Rowlands Gill and 29 via Whickham) also plied between Consett and Newcastle once an hour. This intensive service contrasted with about a dozen trains on weekdays, and two on Sundays. Annual ticket bookings at Consett station in 1930 had slumped to only 14,973, less than a fifth of the volume of 1913.

Although Consett station was not directly affected, two of the lines that converged at Blackhill – from Tow Law and Durham – closed to passengers on 1 May 1939. Passenger numbers at Consett continued to dwindle, and the train service was reduced. The first British Railways timetable (summer 1948) showed only four weekday trains via Annfield Plain to Newcastle (five on Saturdays) and one on Sundays. In the opposite direction there were five weekday trains, with none on Sundays. Public timetables traditionally presented two separate tables, Blackhill-Consett-Newcastle (via Annfield Plain) and Consett-Blackhill-Newcastle (via Lintz Green), and it was not made clear how many services travelled over both lines. From the summer of 1948 the tables were combined to indicate that some trains operated a circular service, so Consett passengers apparently had a greater selection of trains and could choose the slightly shorter journey to Newcastle via Blackhill (17½ as opposed to 19½ miles). By 1951 passenger bookings had dropped to 6,279 from Consett, and 4,122 from Blackhill. On 1 February 1954 the Blackhill to Newcastle via Lintz Green line closed, leaving Consett with an infrequent service of three trains to and from Newcastle on Mondays to Fridays and four on Saturdays. By the summer of 1950 the Sunday train had ceased to run. On 23 May 1955 passenger services between Blackhill and Ouston Junction were withdrawn and Consett station closed. While the other stations on this line were soon demolished, including West Stanley and Annfield Plain in May-June 1965, Consett survived almost intact well into the 1970s. Goods facilities were retained until 2 October 1967, after which there was only a public delivery siding provided.

The route through Consett was popular with enthusiasts who relished the sight (and sound) of steam locomotives battling against the gradient to haul iron-ore trains up to Consett, usually with the assistance of a banking engine. In the later days of steam, 9F 2-10-0 engines headed and banked the trains, with Class 'O1' 2-8-0s and 'Q7' 0-8-0s occasionally deputising on banking duties. From November 1966 diesels took over all operations, but their struggle to reach Consett with their heavy load continued to attract attention. At Consett the steelworks had its own fleet of tank engines until the 1950s, later giving way to Hunslet 0-6-0 diesels; these operated as far as the sidings beside the station.

By the 1970s Consett steelworks had become a remarkable example of geographical inertia; local mining of ore had long ceased, and coal-mining was in terminal decline, yet steel production continued in a recently modernised plant, necessitating the long, uphill journeys of raw material and fuel. In September 1980, in the face of intense local opposition, steel-making came to an end, and almost 3,000 jobs were lost. Although the population of Consett was in decline, it was one of the largest towns in Great Britain without passenger rail access, and local people believed that restoration of the train service could have a role in shoring up the area's post-industrial economy. The line had been maintained to a high standard for the heavy mineral trains and was left in place to carry materials away from the steel site and rails from the extensive sidings. Calls to retain the line fell on deaf ears, however, and the last train, a special rail tour organised by the Derwentside Rail Action Group, visited Consett on 17 March 1984. Rails were soon removed, but the trackbed is one of many in County Durham that, thanks to the vision and enterprise of the County Council, is maintained as a footpath – the Consett & Sunderland Railway Path. It also forms part of the C2C (Coast-to-Coast) cycle route. However, nothing remains of Consett station, or of the hundreds of acres of sidings and the steelworks upon which the town depended.

Consett: On 19 April 1984 two youths and a dog can walk safely beside the disused sidings, soon to be removed. The final special passenger train to Consett had run a month earlier, on 17 March. *Alan Young*

Date opened	14 December 1898
Location	West of roundabout where Seafield Road meets Main Street (B1340)
Company on opening	North Sunderland Railway
Date closed to passengers	29 October 1951
Date closed completely	29 October 1951
Company on closing	North Sunderland Railway
Present state	Demolished; site occupied by car park
County	Northumberland
OS Grid Ref	NU218321

Seahouses was the terminus of a 4-mile branch from Chathill on the East Coast Main Line. This was one of Britain's oddest railways: its birth, operation, and even the nature of its passing were unusual.

The Newcastle & Berwick Railway bypassed Seahouses, which developed in the late 19th century as a small fishing port. The North Eastern Railway also showed no interest in serving the village, so the Trustees of Lord Crewe (the major local landowners) led a campaign for a line to be built to serve the port. They also considered creating a resort – St Aidan's-on-the-Sea – between Seahouses and Bamburgh. A Private Bill (1892) resulted in the North Sunderland Railway Act (North Sunderland being the parish in which Seahouses was located).

The standard-gauge, single-track railway ran almost directly between Chathill and Seahouses. In 1898 the NSR obtained permission to extend to Bamburgh, under the Light Railways Act (1896) – this was never built – and construct and operate the Chathill-Seahouses route as a Light Railway too. This Act enabled railways to be built in regions with limited traffic potential, but where economic growth might be stimulated and communities could benefit from improved access. Light railways had less stringent regulations and signalling arrangements and could be constructed more cheaply. The North Sunderland Railway was possibly the first built under the Act.

Fund-raising for construction was slow. Lord Armstrong, of Bamburgh Castle, contributed, and supported the Bamburgh extension.

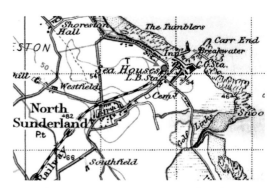

Seahouses, 1947

Savings were made by Light Railway designation, abandoning plans for Fleetham station, and by persuading the NER to allow the NSR to share Chathill station; the up platform would have a bay behind for Seahouses trains. Goods services began on 1 August 1898, with passenger services following on 18 December, after improvements had been made to satisfy the Board of Trade. There was one intermediate station at North Sunderland, which opened with the line but was not included in public timetables until 1934.

The route crossed gently undulating countryside, and gradients nowhere exceeded 1 in 80. Much of the journey was through shallow cuttings or on low embankments.

NSR passenger trains connected with NER trains. The NER agreed to maintain a 'local' stopping service to Chathill and arranged for certain express trains to call. The 1898 branch service was seven trains each way, taking 15 minutes for the journey. The number of trains

Seahouses: Manning Wardle 0-6-0 saddle tank *Bamburgh* with two ex-NER coaches stands at the station in the 1920s. *Peter E. Baughan collection*

hardly changed over the years, with about six each way per day, though in 1915 there were only four daily 'up' workings. Timings changed to keep in line with connecting ECML trains. Sunday trains, introduced in 1934, ceased during the Second World War. From 1939 the journey time on the branch was extended to 20 minutes when a 15mph speed limit was introduced because of the poor condition of the track.

The single platform and station building at Seahouses were north-west of the track. The platform was of ash and tarmac with stone edging. The station building was a simple, single-storey corrugated-iron structure with a pitched roof. It contained the station master's and booking offices; waiting room and parcels office; ladies' waiting room and lavatory; and (in an 'extension') the gentlemen's lavatory. The station master's office/booking office extended the full depth of the building, but the remaining sections were recessed, so the roof served as an open shelter. Oil lighting gave way to electricity in 1926. The trackwork included an extension of the passenger line into the engine shed, and south-east of the passenger platform were a run-round loop and two sidings, one serving the fish loading area. The other was a public siding with coal pens (not coal drops), a crane and a warehouse. The NSR could not afford to build a house for the first station master, who had to make do with subsidised lodgings. Signals were installed only at Chathill and at Seahouses, where there were ground signals; ground frames sufficed for operating the sidings points.

The company's first locomotive, the 0-6-0 Manning Wardle saddle tank *Bamburgh*, was acquired on hire-purchase. It gave almost half a century's service, expiring four years before the line itself. The five original coaches were cast-off Highland Railway four-wheelers, but within their first week of NSR service they were sold to the Yorkshire Wagon & Finance Company to raise cash to pay the contractor. These coaches were used until 1911-13, then replaced with 30-year-old ex-NER stock. In 1937 three ex-Great Eastern six-wheel coaches were acquired. Goods wagons were lent to the North Sunderland Railway by the NER/LNER. However, the NSR created improvised stone trucks by decapitating two Highland Railway coaches.

In the 1930s, economising wherever possible, the NSR neglected track maintenance, and experimented with diesel traction. An Armstrong-Whitworth diesel-electric shunter successfully operated passenger and mixed trains in 1933-34, so a similar locomotive was bought, to be named *The Lady Armstrong*. She proved unreliable and was abandoned in 1946.

With only one, or at best two, locomotives, the NSR relied from time to time on help from NER, LNER and BR motive power. These included a Class 'H2' 0-6-0 tank, LNER 'J79', and finally a 'Y7' 0-4-0; when the latter was unavailable in the autumn of 1948, the NSR provided taxis for passengers.

Even before 1914, motor-car competition was apparent, but the NSR carried about 20,000 passengers a year in the mid-1920s. Goods traffic (chiefly coal and salt to Seahouses, and fish in the opposite direction) halved between 1910 and the mid-1920s.

The NSR depended heavily upon the NER, the LNER, and later BR(NE). The main line conveyed passengers to and from the branch, operated Chathill station, and issued tickets to North Sunderland and Seahouses. The NER/LNER and BR manufactured the tickets issued at North Sunderland and Seahouses. Until 1936 excursions visited Seahouses, an NSR locomotive hauling main-line coaches from Chathill. Wagons and locomotives were supplied, when required, by the main-line operator. However, these favours came at a price. The NSR's debts to the LNER mounted until 1939, when the LNER took control, although the NSR officially remained independent. After nationalisation in 1948 the NSR continued its ambiguous existence, independent in name but reliant upon the British Transport Commission for motive power.

Financial difficulties reached a head in July 1951 when the BTC advised the NSR that the 1939 LNER/NSR operating agreement was to be cancelled, and motive power withdrawn. The condition of the NSR track – still limited to a painfully slow 15mph – was such that only one obsolete class of BR(NE) locomotive could safely use it. The coaches were life-expired. The BTC operated the United Chathill-Seahouses buses, duplicating the railway service, and could carry the railway mail traffic. BR road services could carry parcels and goods, operating between Chathill or Belford, Seahouses, and other villages.

The final train left Seahouses at 4.20pm on Saturday 27 October 1951, behind Class 'Y7' locomotive No 68089. It carried an unofficial 'Farne Islander' headboard. The day's three later trains were cancelled, with taxis run instead. The official closure date for all traffic was 29 October 1951, and track-lifting took place in 1953. The North Sunderland Light Railway was formally wound up on 16 June 1952. To avoid an Act of Parliament being required allowing sale of assets, the NSR was registered on 25 April 1952 as the North Sunderland Light Railway Co Ltd. Thus for almost two months – after the line closed – its name acknowledged that it had been a 'Light Railway'! After closure, the former station master acted as agent for BR and British Road Services in the Seahouses station building, while BRS used the warehouse. Although much of the trackbed is still visible as a line of trees and bushes separating fields, by the early 1970s the station site had been transformed into a car park.

Seahouses: The derelict station looking south-west in 1959, eight years after closure. *John Mann collection*

FONTBURN HALT (1904)

Date opened	1 June 1904 (officially)
Location	Alongside track leading north from Fontburn Reservoir; station had no road access
Company on opening	North British Railway
Date closed to passengers	15 September 1952
Date closed completely	11 November 1963 (as Ewesley Siding)
Company on closing	British Railways (North Eastern Region)
Present state	Wooden platform has gone, but fence posts at back of platform remain, including taller post that held oil lantern.
County	Northumberland
OS Grid Ref	NZ051942

Fontburn was one of only five public 'Halts' in the North Eastern Region of British Railways. Brinkburn and Lewiefield – which, like Fontburn, were on the former North British lines in Northumberland – and North Eastrington and Springhead – on the former Hull & Barnsley Railway – were the others. A 'halt' is difficult to define precisely, but it was generally unstaffed, with short platforms (sometimes no platforms) and with basic shelters, if any. This obscure and remote halt on the Rothbury branch had a remarkable history.

In 1859 the Wansbeck Valley Railway obtained powers to build a line between Morpeth and Reedsmouth, and the eastern section between Morpeth and Scotsgap opened in July 1862. Three grandees who supported the Wansbeck scheme – Richard Hodgson, Earl Grey, and Sir W. C. Trevelyan – threw their weight behind the Northumberland Central Railway project, which obtained an Act in 1863 to build a line from Scotsgap, via Rothbury and Wooler, to the Berwick-Kelso line at Cornhill.

By February 1864 sufficient capital had been raised to construct the line between Scotsgap and Rothbury but not for the remainder, and, despite efforts to raise further capital, the route beyond Rothbury was abandoned by a further Act on 12 April 1867. The 13-mile branch to Rothbury ceremonially opened for public traffic on 1 November 1870, with intermediate stations at Rothley (private), Ewesley and Brinkburn. From the outset the North British

Railway provided the service, in conjunction with the Morpeth-Scotsgap line. Unfortunately the NCR was in serious debt. The reduction of the through route to a branch with little earning potential dulled the NBR's enthusiasm to acquire the line; nevertheless, on 1 February 1872 the NBR absorbed the NCR. The NBR made a number of improvements. Rothley opened to the public in 1873 and was renamed Longwitton in April 1875, and the terminus at Rothbury was substantially improved. Sidings and branches were built to serve lineside industries and small collieries. In 1881 the NBR supported a proposal to extend to Wooler, but this came to nothing, and the Rothbury branch remained a peaceful, rural line.

The branch was built as single track, but sufficient land was purchased for doubling, should the need arise. It crossed hilly terrain, requiring steep gradients, numerous curves and substantial earthworks. A 50-foot embankment at Forestburn and a deep cutting at Thrum Mill, near Rothbury, were constructed. A 12-arch viaduct, about 60 feet high (and still intact), crossed Font Burn. From Scotsgap there was a 1 in 75 climb to the 694-foot summit at Longwitton, and a 1 in 60 descent between Brinkburn and Rothbury.

Fontburn was a later addition to the branch. By 1896 trains possibly called unofficially for workers at Whitehouse Quarry and limeworks and for occupants of railway cottages. A contemporary Ordnance Survey map shows what appears to be a short platform near the quarry sidings. From 1901 to 1909 construction of Fontburn Reservoir required a temporary village for about 450 people beside the railway. Various 3-foot-gauge lines served the construction site, and associated sidings were built from the Rothbury branch. The NBR provided a passenger station, west of the track, with an 80-yard timber platform, waiting shed and booking office. This opened on 12 January 1903 as the 'Temporary Platform at Whitehouse Siding' for workmen. Bradshaw included the new station, but removed it when the Board of Trade complained that it had not been inspected. Duly inspected, Whitehouse was reinstated. On 1 May 1904 it was renamed Fontburn to avoid confusion with Whitehouse, Aberdeenshire. After the construction workers left, the station was retained, but it closed to passengers on 3 October 1921, and its goods facility was renamed Ewesley Siding. In response to a local petition, Fontburn reopened, unstaffed, on 21 November 1921 as Fontburn Halt, and the nameboard was altered accordingly. Passengers obtained tickets from the guard or at Scotsgap or Rothbury stations. Ewesley's station master took charge of the halt.

Fontburn's train service until the Second World War amounted to three departures in each direction on weekdays, with two coaches generally sufficing, or a single coach in the final years when the service was reduced to two trains in each direction. In LNER and BR days branch trains were hauled by 'G5' and 'J21' locomotives, based at Rothbury. Passenger traffic on the branch dwindled, particularly when buses began to operate to Rothbury, which, with a population of 1,648 in 1951, was the only village directly served by the railway. In the same year only 2,603 tickets were issued at Rothbury, but unfortunately no figures are available for Fontburn or the other branch stations. In harsh winter weather when snow blocked the roads the railway was a lifeline, but this was not considered sufficient reason to maintain the passenger service, which ended on 15 September

Above **Fontburn Halt:** On 13 September 1952 passengers alight from the 4.30pm Rothbury to Morpeth service. This was the final train from Rothbury on the last day of passenger services. *J.W. Armstrong, Armstrong Railway Photographic Trust*

Below **Fontburn Halt:** In March 2006 the platform site is discernable as an earth mound. The stone-built access path and the concrete post with lamp bracket can be compared with the 1952 view. *Nick Catford*

1952. Occasional excursions continued to visit the branch, some steam-hauled, others DMU-operated. A farewell steam excursion visited Rothbury on 9 November 1963, two days before goods services ended. The very last passenger train was a private diesel working in July 1964 carrying the North Eastern Region's Chief Civil Engineer's staff on their annual works outing. The tracks were lifted later that year.

MANORS NORTH (1909)

Date opened	1 January 1909
Location	Immediately south of New Bridge Street and east of Central Motorway East, A167(M). Technopole Business Park occupies much of station site.
Company on opening	North Eastern Railway
Date closed to passengers	23 January 1978; entrance building continued to give access to Manors East platforms for some years.
Date closed completely	23 January 1978
Company on closing	British Rail (Eastern Region)
Present state	Demolished
County	Northumberland (now Tyne & Wear)
OS Grid Ref	NZ253644

Known by local people as 'The Manors', the name refers to the area on the edge of Newcastle's city centre that was almost obliterated by the station as it grew into an extravagant nine-platform affair. Passengers travelling from Newcastle towards Benton gained a vivid impression of the station's vastness, as first the 'Coast Circle' via Wallsend platforms (8 and 9) curved away, followed by the East Coast Main Line platforms (6 and 7), before the train drew in to platform 1, with numbers 2 (for trains from Benton to Newcastle) and 3 to 5 (for Blyth and Newbiggin services) to the right. Today a short island platform on the East Coast Main Line is all that remains. From 1909 until 1969 Manors was officially two separate stations – East and North – but the latter closed in 1978, justifying its inclusion as a 'lost station'.

Manors North: The exterior in June 1969. *John Mann*

An Act of Parliament on 21 June 1836 authorised the construction of the Newcastle & North Shields Railway (N&NS), which opened on 20 June 1839. The Newcastle terminus was intended to be at Pilgrim Street but, owing to the possibility of a central Newcastle station being provided for all railways serving the city,

the N&NS ended a short distance to the north-east. A temporary terminus opened close to Carliol Square; known as 'Newcastle', this was effectively the first Manors (East) station. Its buildings were not finished until 1842. In July 1846 the Newcastle & Berwick Railway (N&B) absorbed the N&NS, and used the existing North Shields route for about 1½ miles to Heaton Junction for its line, which opened as far as Morpeth on 1 March 1847. From another junction on the east side of Trafalgar Street the N&B pushed further into the city centre, to a junction with the Newcastle and Darlington

Above **Manors North:** Looking north in June 1969, we see the bay Platforms 3 and 4, formerly used by Newbiggin trains, and Platforms 1 and 2, used by trains via Benton. *John Mann*

Right **Manors North:** A general view, looking south from Platform 1 in June 1973. *Alan Young*

line at the new Central station on 30 August 1850. The former 'Manors' terminus was retained as a coal depot, and a new through station was constructed above Trafalgar Street, on the site of the later platforms 6 and 7. This had an office building on the down side, in the angle of the junction. Access between platforms was through one of the arches of the new viaduct. The platforms were extended and given extensive roofing in 1872-73.

In 1864 the Blyth & Tyne Railway (B&T) entered Newcastle from the north, opening its New Bridge Street terminus about 300 yards north of Manors. This station would eventually, in 1909, be superseded by Manors (North). The

North Eastern Railway (NER), which absorbed the York, Newcastle & Berwick Railway (as the N&B had become) in 1854, went on, 20 years later, to absorb the B&T. Despite owning the two neighbouring stations, the NER was slow to link them. To do so would require the demolition of Trafalgar goods station, and there was already a link between the two routes at Benton.

As traffic grew, the 2 miles between Newcastle and Heaton, through Manors, became congested. In 1887 the route was quadrupled, and Manors was remodelled. The

old down platform and building were retained (as Platform 1) but a long island platform (2 and 3, later renumbered 7 and 8) replaced the old up one, and Platform 4 (later 9) was added, its tall, three-storey curving frontage following the line of Melbourne Street. Shop units occupied the street-level space, with waiting rooms at platform level. The enlarged station required a labyrinth of passages and stairways beneath it – likened by one reviewer to the fictional castle Gormenghast! Access to the platform from Melbourne Street involved the ascent of a lengthy staircase; part way up, a tunnel led off to the other platforms. Robust, slate-and-glass canopies were carried on ornate Gothic columns and spandrel brackets. Platforms 2 and 3 (later 7 and 8) had ridge-and-furrow roofing with hipped ends, carried on two lines of columns, sheltering a timber office range including a booking office, towards its south-western end, and waiting rooms. On Platform 4 (later 9) the roof ridge ran along the platform. Quadrupling of the line between Manors and Central Station was completed in 1894.

The next significant development was beside the railway rather than on it. In 1901 Manors power station opened to supply electricity to the city's tramway system. This competition stimulated not only the electrification of the existing lines between the city and the coast but also the eventual construction of the Manors-New Bridge Street link with new platforms at

Manors East: At 16.26 on 4 July 1973 a train from Newcastle, running via the Riverside branch to Monkseaton – and ultimately to Newcastle – arrives at Platform 8. Although Manors East is not a 'lost station', it now possesses only a shortened island platform used by local trains on the East Coast Main Line. *Alan Young*

Manors (North), which opened on 1 July 1909.

The extensions to Manors were on a generous scale. Two through platforms (1 and 2) and three bays (3, 4 and 5) made up Manors North; the older platforms became Manors East, numbered 6 to 9. The new line came across the corner of Trafalgar Street bridge on girders, then over the site of the Newcastle & Berwick station building, which was replaced with an office range adjoining Platform 1. The North station building, approached from Trafalgar Street, was set back behind a wide, triangular forecourt. The core of the building – the booking hall – was a single-storey structure in red brick with a hipped roof, fronted by a large gable and surmounted by a clock cupola. Passengers entered from the forecourt at the north side of the booking hall under a small glazed awning. From the booking hall a staircase led down to a subway to Platforms 2 and 3, from which Platforms 4, 5 and 6 were then directly accessible; a parcels subway and lifts were also provided. A footbridge also linked all platforms, stretching from the up end of Platform 1 to the

Manors North: Trains between Tynemouth and Newcastle via Benton were to be withdrawn on 8 January 1978 for Metro construction work, and on that date a DMU leaves Platform 2 for Newcastle direct. In fact the service continued for a further fortnight. Platform 7 (Manors East) is in the background. *Alan Young*

down end of Platform 9. There was access to the station from the New Bridge Street overbridge at the north end of Platforms 1 and 2. A long, covered ramp delivered passengers to the exterior of the main building, while covered flights of stairs led to Platform 2/3. This facility was possibly already disused when it was damaged by fire in the early 1960s. Extensive glazed roofing sheltered the new platforms, supported by columns with Ionic capitals and spandrels embellished with the City of Newcastle's 'Three Castle' crest. The new station roofing lent a light, airy atmosphere to Manors North, in contrast to the more gloomy platforms of Manors East. William Bell was Chief Architect of the North Eastern Railway from 1877 until 1914, when these major changes were made to Manors station. Lavish new buildings featuring large expanses of glazed roofing at Monkseaton, Whitley

Bay and Tynemouth, on the Coast line from Manors, were also impressive products of Bell's office; unlike Manors North, they survive to be admired today.

As noted earlier, electrification of the Newcastle tramways spurred the NER to 'fight the devil with fire', and the company electrified the route from Newcastle Central to New Bridge Street via Wallsend/Carville and Tynemouth using a 600V DC third-rail system, also increasing the frequency of the service. From 1909 electric trains were introduced through the new Manors North, travelling to Benton, but the 'Coast Circle' electric service, starting and terminating at Central station, did not begin until 1917. Electric services continued until 17 June 1967, diesel multiple units having been gradually phased in during the previous year to replace the fleet of electric trains that had operated since 1937. Although in practice one station – the nameboards

Manors: The layout of the North and East stations. *Alan Young*

Manors North:
Looking south from New Bridge Street in December 1979, the platform roofing has been removed from island bay Platforms 4/5, and Platforms 2/3 await similar treatment. *Alan Young*

bore the name 'Manors' – the old and new parts were officially Manors East and North from 1 January 1909 until 20 February 1969. Some tickets referred to East and North, as did LNER timetables until June 1947. In British Railways days working timetables still distinguished East from North. Public timetables indicated by footnotes that express services from Monkseaton via the East Coast Main Line called at the East rather than the North platforms.

On a typical weekday in the early 1960s, outside rush hours, an electric multiple unit called every 20 minutes to the coast via Benton (Platform 1), and to the coast via Wallsend (Platform 8), and from the coast via Benton (Platform 2) and from the coast via Wallsend (Platform 9), totalling 12 services per hour. Rush-hour Coast Circle services were frequent but at irregular intervals, and occasional services to and from the Riverside branch (via Carville) and Blyth/Newbiggin used the station too. On Saturdays the Blyth/Newbiggin services operated at hourly intervals, terminating in Platforms 3, 4 or 5, rather than using Central station. By the early 1960s these were diesel multiple units, though the first working of the day – originating at Newcastle Central, travelling to Newbiggin, then returning to Manors – was steam-hauled and conveyed mail and parcels. Platforms 6 and 7 had irregular express EMU workings to and from the coast via the East

Coast Main Line and Benton SE Curve, as well as DMUs to and from Alnwick. Some steam- or diesel-hauled 'semi-fast' Berwick and Edinburgh services called at Manors, but main-line expresses did not. A variety of goods traffic also passed through the station, and goods services on the three-quarter-mile Quayside branch, electrified with overhead equipment – but third-rail in and just outside its tunnels – terminated here. (The Quayside branch changed to diesel haulage on 29 February 1964 and closed on 16 June 1969. For many years thereafter, poles to support the electric wiring remained on Manors East platforms.)

The variety of passenger services began to decline when, on 2 November 1964, Blyth/Newbiggin trains were withdrawn, making Platforms 3 to 5 at Manors North redundant. The few Riverside branch trains ceased from 23 July 1973. Much more significantly, trains were withdrawn permanently from Manors North when the coast service via Benton ended on 23 January 1978 in preparation for Metro works; coast trains via Wallsend continued to use Manors East until 11 August 1980. On 14 November 1982 a regular local passenger service resumed at Manors, but using the new underground Metro station on the Newcastle to Coast route.

Until the mid-1970s Manors was busy and well maintained; 201,173 tickets were issued in

1967, increasing in 1972 to 346,217 when the Coast Circle services were revitalised in the 'Tynerider' promotion of 1970. Hanging baskets adorned North's Platforms 1 and 2 in the summer months. The North Eastern Region's favourite 'oriental blue' paint was applied to iron columns and woodwork – though this did not really blend with the tangerine signage! LNER electric 'mint imperial'-design lamps hung from the roofing of the North station, or were carried on hooped standards on the open platforms. Small LNER name tablets accompanied the lamps; tangerine BR totem signs were, sadly, never fitted. Under the East station roofing the electric lighting had LNER brick-shaped diffusers bearing the station name. Tall, vandal-proof lamps arrived in 1971, and 'corporate identity' black-and-white signage followed in 1973.

From August 1980 only some 30 local services on the East Coast Main Line called at Manors. The number dwindled through the 1990s and by 2010 the service at Manors was almost annihilated; however, in the summer of 2011 a respectable hourly-interval Monday-Friday service was introduced.

Manors North: The buildings on Platform 1 are in an advanced stage of dilapidation in September 1985, but passengers enter the station, through the rubble, to reach the operating 'East' Platforms 7/8. The BR(NE) oriental blue paint still adorns the redundant iron columns. *Alan Young*

The near-extinction of Manors's passenger services was accompanied by a dramatic contraction of the station. By late 1979 the tracks had been removed from North station, and demolition of the buildings was advanced. In the spring of 1980 the only old buildings remaining were on 'local' Platforms 1 and 9. Northbound main-line passengers had to make do with a crude, breezeblock shelter, while southbound passengers – if there were any – and coast-bound passengers, who shared Platforms 7 and 8, had to shelter in the subway. In September 1985 the once-dignified entrance building on Platform 1 was being demolished. The cupola, stripped of its clock, rose proudly above the crumbling remains of the booking hall. On the façade a tangerine 'British Railways Manors' sign was still fixed to the gable in front of the turret, accompanied by a modern British

Rail sign, reassuring doubters that trains still called. Access to the station was gained by a lengthy footbridge over the 'Central Motorway East'. On reaching the unstaffed station the would-be passenger had to navigate the roofless North booking hall, avoiding chunks of fallen masonry, then continue along the rubble-strewn former Platform 1, overhung by roofing supports awaiting demolition. Beyond this a causeway crossed the old trackbed to Platform 2. To catch a train to Newcastle Central a footbridge then had to be crossed. By 1985 Platforms 2 to 5 had gone, and much of their site had been landscaped. The platform-level buildings and awnings on Platform 9 were removed in 1986.

By 1991 Manors (East) possessed one shortened island platform, with overhead wires installed for the main-line electrification. The Technopole Business Park on the site of Manors North, and extending into the space between the North and East stations, might have been expected to justify an improved train service at the surviving platform, but the frequent services at the nearby Manors Metro underground station probably met workers' needs.

In recent years Manors station has attracted much interest, with lively blog-site discussions on its every feature. Perhaps the use of its gloomy subway and staircases as a location for the 1971 cult movie *Get Carter*, starring Michael Caine, is part of its mystique. Contributors are amazed that so little remains of such a vast and formerly important transport facility. The clock cupola survives, but it is in South Shields as a feature of the Marsden Rattler pub.

Manors North: Looking north in July 1991, fragments of Platforms 1 and 2 are in the foreground while the framework of an office building in Technopole Business Park is being constructed across much of the station site. *Alan Young*

DARRAS HALL (1913)

Date opened	1 October 1913
Location	North-east of former level crossing on Broadway. Old Station Court is adjacent to site, and trackbed is footpath and cycle route.
Company on opening	North Eastern Railway
Date closed to passengers	17 June 1929
Date closed completely	2 August 1954
Company on closing	Passenger services: London & North Eastern Railway Goods services: British Railways (North Eastern Region)
Present state	Demolished
County	Northumberland
OS Grid Ref	NZ152714

In its rural setting south-west of Ponteland, Darras Hall estate developed from 1907 when a group of Newcastle businessmen bought a large plot of land with the aim of creating a 'garden city' for professional and managerial men and their families. A century on, the founders would be delighted that it has become one of the most select residential areas in

Darras Hall: This undated view is looking south-east after closure to passengers, with the wooden platform and buildings still in a reasonable state of repair. *J. W. Armstrong, Armstrong Railway Photographic Trust*

Darras Hall: This view from April 1977 shows the platform elevation. The verandah and the 'half-timber' decoration remain intact almost 50 years after closure, but – despite the enviable reputation of the estate – graffiti-writers have been at work. At this time the building was in use as a church. *Alan Young*

northern England, with its tree-lined avenues concealing opulent properties – exclusive and expensive enough to be considered worthy residences by Premier League footballers.

In 1896 the North Eastern Railway promoted the Ponteland Light Railway, branching from the Newcastle-Whitley Bay route at South Gosforth (then known as Gosforth) into an area lacking passenger lines. The Light Railways Act (1896) encouraged the British network to extend into areas with limited traffic potential, but where economic growth might be stimulated and isolated communities could benefit from better access. Light railways had more relaxed regulations and could be built more cheaply, for instance by using lighter rails and less ballast.

Construction began in 1900. The 6¾-mile route was through gently undulating countryside beyond Newcastle's built-up area, and earthworks were relatively light. There

were several level crossings over public roads, but major roads and mineral lines were crossed by bridges. Goods services began on 1 March 1905, and passenger services on 1 June. It was intended to electrify the route as an extension to the 'Coast Circle'; however, only the east end of the line was electrified for access to Gosforth Car Sheds from 1923. (Further electrification was delayed for more than 50 years!) Operation of branch services was generally by Fletcher 'BTP' locomotives fitted with auto apparatus, based at Heaton shed. Advertised as 'steam auto-cars', these push-and-pulls provided nine to ten services between South Gosforth and Ponteland on weekdays (four on Sundays), taking 20 minutes to complete the journey. By June 1920 Sunday trains had been withdrawn.

In November 1908 the NER deposited plans with Parliament for a 1¼-mile extension to Darras Hall under the name of the Little Callerton Railway. Unlike the parent branch to Ponteland, this route was not a Light Railway. The extension was to serve the residential area where development was just beginning. Parliamentary approval was granted in 1909, and the Estate entered into an Agreement with the NER on 18 October 1910 for railway access. The single track was largely on an embankment, and sufficient space was available for the addition of a second track should traffic warrant it. Goods services to Darras Hall started on 27 September 1913, followed by passenger trains on 1 October. The trains operated between South Gosforth and Darras Hall with a reversal at Ponteland – a simple manoeuvre for the 'auto-cars'. The Darras Hall extension was a financial failure. The estate grew slowly, and its loose grid of roads, with detached houses at a maximum density of six per acre, limited the number of potential passengers. By June 1920 the scanty provision of three trains per day, and the need to change at South Gosforth, must have been a disincentive to use the service. No industrial development was permitted at Darras Hall, apart from the NER goods yard, so even goods traffic was restricted.

Darras Hall station was 1 mile 20½ chains from the junction at Ponteland. Two tracks passed through the station, but there was only a single timber platform on the up line. The building, like its neighbours on the South Gosforth-Ponteland branch, was wooden, but the design was more elaborate to satisfy the exacting standards of the local residents. The single-storey main building had twin pavilions; their gable ends, together with the main gables, were decorated with a Tudoresque striped 'half-timber' design. Between the pavilions was a lean-to awning, supported by six pillars. There was also a smaller wooden building on the platform. The layout of the station was (like Ponteland) not typical of a terminus, and although there were no explicit plans to extend the branch when it was opened, it was later extended, for coal traffic, to Belsay Colliery.

As for the original Ponteland branch, following a promising start Newcastle Corporation buses (which also served Darras Hall) snatched the traffic from the trains. The introduction of Sentinel Steam Cars, running through to Newcastle, failed to revive the traffic, and housing development along the route was limited. So it was that the Ponteland and Darras Hall line was closed as early as 1929. Ponteland

enjoyed a passenger service for 24 years, and Darras Hall for only 16. Parcels traffic ceased to be handled on 5 January 1935, but goods traffic continued. From time to time the branch provided a serene retreat where the Royal Train could pass the night, until Darras Hall closed to all traffic in 1954. Ponteland's goods service ended in 1967, and the rails were lifted beyond Prestwick ICI explosives factory siding, north of Callerton; this facility closed in 1989.

After a gap of more than 50 years much of the Ponteland branch regained its passenger trains in 1981 when the route from South Gosforth to Bank Foot (Kenton) reopened, and was finally electrified, as part of the Metro network. The service was extended to Newcastle Airport on 17 November 1991, which involved a short branch from the Ponteland route. It is unlikely that the Metro will extend to Ponteland – and even less likely that Darras Hall will return to the railway map.

The Darras Hall branch had a short-lived extension to Belsay Colliery, 4 miles south-south-west of Belsay village in the depths of the Northumbrian countryside. The colliery opened in 1923, and the 7½-mile single-track railway in 1927. The line was known as the Wallridge Mineral Railway after the sparsely inhabited parish where it terminated; the population in 1901 was two, and in 1931 there were 37 inhabitants. The workforce never reached 100, production was limited, and the colliery closed in 1930. An untimetabled passenger train service for miners ran between the colliery and Wallridge, where a short platform served miners' cottages. Motive power was an ex-Glasgow & South Western Railway 0-6-0, and there were six trucks, two passenger coaches and a guard's van. The railway lay moribund until 1942, when the track was lifted.

After closure Darras Hall station was used as a church, but it was demolished in 1992/93. A footpath and cycle route now follows the Darras Hall branch as well as part of the Wallridge extension.

Date opened	Constructed in 1914; never opened
Location	Within Whitley Bay golf course, close to public footpath that leaves A193 Blyth Road at sharp bend
Company on opening	North Eastern Railway, which built the Collywell Bay branch
Date closed to passengers	Project abandoned on 1 December 1931
Date closed completely	N/A
Company on closing	Abandoned by the London & North Eastern Railway
Present state	Demolished
County	Northumberland (now Tyne & Wear)
OS Grid Ref	NZ341745

Had the outbreak of war in 1914 been delayed for a few months, the coastal village of Seaton Sluice would have become the terminus of an electrified branch line from Monkseaton, and the intermediate station at Brierdene would undoubtedly have been surrounded by housing. Instead, the Collywell Bay branch line – almost ready to be opened – remained in suspended animation for 17 years before being abandoned. Tantalising fragments of the line survive, and can readily be seen on aerial photographs.

When the Blyth & Tyne Railway's 'Avenue Branch' opened to passengers in 1861 between Hartley, Whitley/Monkseaton and Tynemouth

Brierdene: These images of how the station building might have looked – had it been constructed – were compiled by Bill Fawcett, based on engineers' drawings from 1923. *Bill Fawcett*

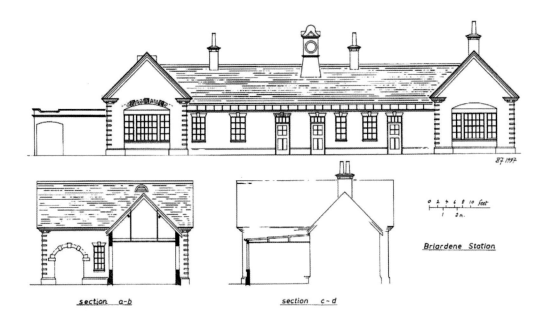

87 1997

0 2 4 6 8 10 feet
1   3 m.

Briardene Station

section a-b

section c-d

it bypassed Seaton Sluice, and continued southwards, part of its length following the course of Whitley Wagonway. It was not until the early years of the 20th century, when housing development seemed likely at Seaton Sluice, that plans were devised by the North Eastern Railway to put the village on the railway map. (For a brief spell in 1851-53 passengers could reach the village using trains on a colliery wagonway.) Following electrification of the Newcastle-Whitley Bay 'Coast Circle' in 1904, a Bill to enable the construction of a branch from Monkseaton was deposited in 1910-11, and it received the Royal Assent on 18 August 1911.

A contract was agreed on 14 November 1912 with C. M. Skinner for an electrified branch line to Seaton Sluice, a little under 2 miles in length, leaving the Avenue branch about a mile north of Monkseaton station. This section of the Avenue branch would be doubled, and Monkseaton station would be rebuilt on a grand scale to accommodate Seaton Sluice trains. It was decided not to call the terminus Seaton Sluice, but Collywell Bay, a name considered

Brierdene: This is the unopened station, looking south circa 1930, with the platforms, signal box, footbridge and single track in place. *J. C. Dean collection*

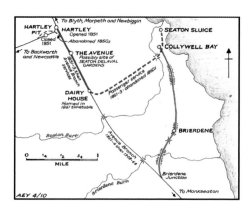

Brierdene: A map of the Collywell Bay and Seaton Sluice branches. *Alan Young*

more appropriate for an aspiring genteel resort and commuter destination. In May 1913 an Agreement was made with Lord Hastings permitting the NER to build the line across his land, of which he was to sell 21½ acres at £40 per acre. It was implied that at least 350 houses would be constructed near the terminus.

An intermediate station with a passing loop on the single-track branch was to be provided at Brierdene, 53 chains from Brierdene Junction

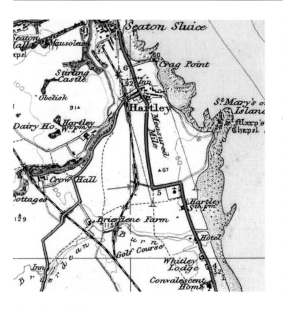

Brierdene, 1919

on the Avenue branch.

The station – referred to as Delaval Bay on a District Engineers' map, and Briardene, or Brierdene Halt, by other sources – was expected to become the heart of a new residential area. As at Collywell Bay, the main building and signal box were to be on the east platform with a waiting shelter on the west platform. The station entrance was planned at the north end of the block, with a glazed verandah, behind which was a glass-roofed booking area that fronted the office. The overall shape of the building was the favoured NER single-storey block with cross-wings at each end clasping a platform verandah with a glazed front. Unlike other NER stations of that era (such as Darras Hall), the building was to be largely of brick rather than timber. A cupola with finial and weathervane was included to add a note of distinction. The platforms were built, connected by a footbridge that was not a standard NER design and had previously been used at the old Monkseaton station. A signal box was partially constructed towards the south end of the east platform, with what was possibly a permanent way hut immediately south of the platform ramp.

The NER intended to open the branch at the beginning of November 1914, and the name Collywell Bay was added to the destination blinds on Tyneside electric trains. Construction had reached an advanced stage when the First

World War broke out in August 1914, and the project was halted. A double line of permanent way was in place as well as the station platforms, bridges and signal boxes. A stretch of electric 'third rail' was laid at the Monkseaton end of the Avenue branch, the signal box at Brierdene Junction was constructed, and the new Monkseaton station was nearing completion; this station opened the following year. On the outbreak of war house-building in the area ceased. In 1916 the Ministry of Munitions and the Railway Executive Committee, faced with a shortage of essential materials, decided that rails could be acquired by singling lightly used lines. In 1917 the rails of the Collywell Bay branch were therefore lifted. However, a stretch of single line 1 mile 1,754 yards long was restored using second-hand track – probably before the end of that year – for a naval coastal defence gun, mounted on a specially built railway wagon.

After the war the local council expected the line to be completed. The LNER reviewed the project in 1924 but did not proceed because little housing development had taken place at Seaton Sluice. In November 1930 the cost of completing the project and operating a half-hourly passenger service and goods trains was weighed against potential revenue, and the outcome was a decision not to proceed; its fate was sealed in an Agreement between the LNER and Lord Hastings on 1 December 1931. The line and bridges were removed by the end of 1932, but Lord Hastings permitted the partially built stations to remain in place because of the expense of their removal. Brierdene's second-hand footbridge found its third home at Byker station on the Riverside branch in Newcastle.

The southern section of the Collywell Bay branch from the Avenue branch (closed in 1964) as far as Brierdene station has been almost obliterated by Whitley Bay golf course, but north of this its course is marked by rough grass and bushes, before disappearing under a housing estate at Seaton Sluice. A bridge abutment survives where the branch crossed Hartley Lane (B1325) together with abutments flanking a footpath just north of the golf course. Collywell Bay's platforms were intact amidst housing in 1964, but have since disappeared.

DISUSED STATIONS
Closed Railway Stations In the UK

S ince its launch in 2004, *Subterranea Britannica's* DISUSED STATIONS web site has become established as one of the most comprehensive online photographic records of closed stations in the UK with a wide selection of 'then' and 'now' photographs.

Each station page includes a selection of archive pictures showing the station before closure and the site as it appears today plus ordnance survey maps, tickets, timetables and a brief history of the station or line.

W ith over 6000 closed station in the UK this will be a very long term project but with 1552 stations covered (as of August 2011) we have already made a serious dent in that number but there is still a long way to go. Disused Stations welcomes contributions from anyone, any station, any line, any period in time but if you aren't the photographer please make sure you have the copyright owner's permission before sending photographs for inclusion on the web site.

Visit us at www.disused-stations.org.uk/sites.shtml
- you won't be disappointed.